Of Silver we have heard no more. That formidable seafaring man with one leg has at last gone clean out of my life; but I dare say he met his old Negress, and perhaps still lives in comfort with her and Captain Flint. It is to be hoped so, I suppose, for his chances of comfort in another world are very small.

**R.L. Stevenson**, *Treasure Island*



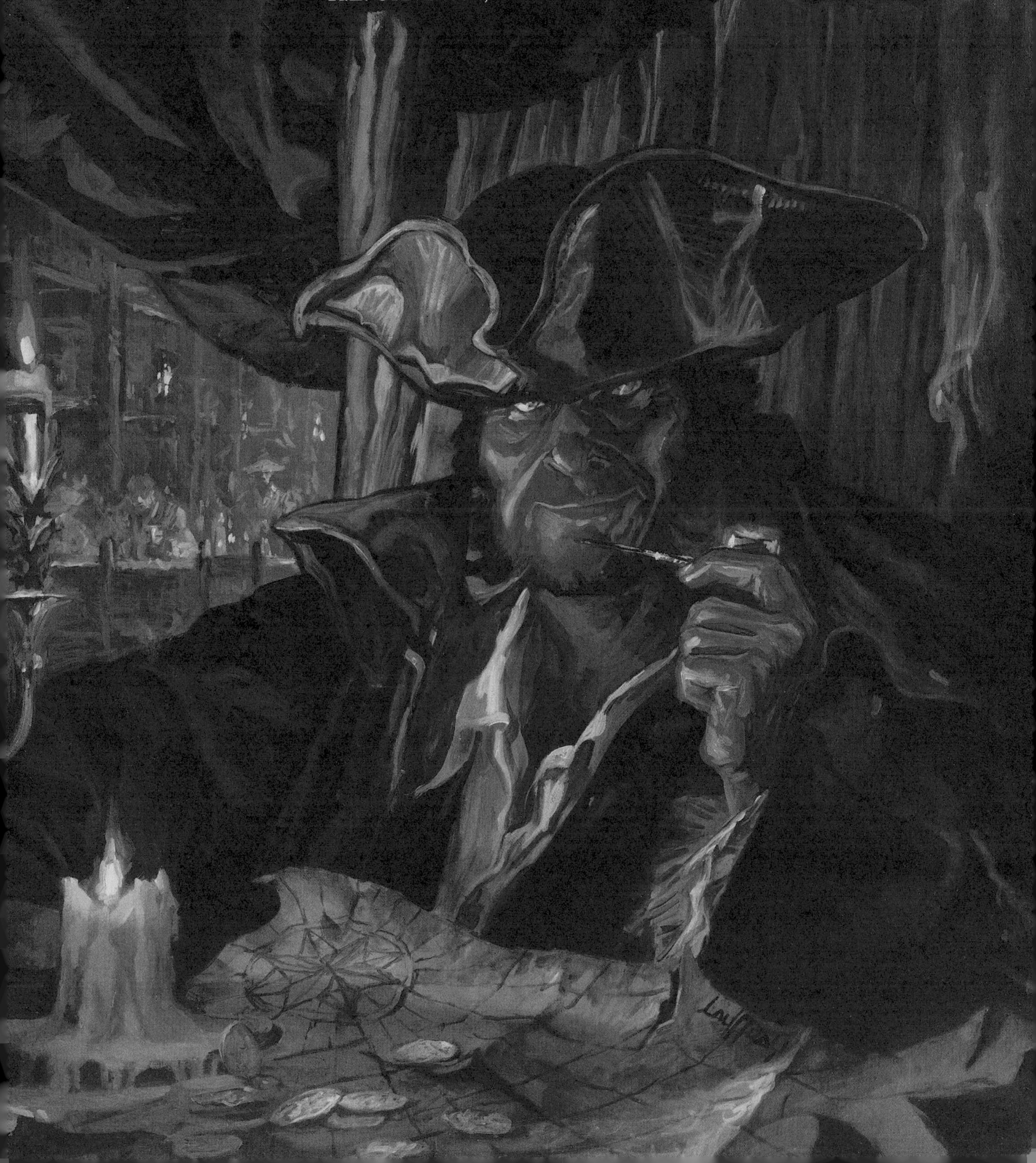

"THE MASTER IS THE ONE WHO EMBRACES THE RISK OF DEATH.
THE SLAVE IS THE ONE WHO THINKS ONLY OF SURVIVING."
GILLES LAPOUGE

THE STORY SO FAR

DEEP INSIDE THE UNEXPLORED LANDS OF THE AMAZON, LORD BYRON HASTINGS HAS DISCOVERED THE CITY OF GUIANA-CAPAC AND ITS FABULOUS WEALTH. IN ORDER TO BRING SOME OF THAT WEALTH BACK TO ENGLAND, HE SENDS THE NATIVE MOXTECHICA WITH A LETTER ASKING HIS WIFE, LADY VIVIAN HASTINGS, TO FUND A SECOND EXPEDITION, AND HIS BROTHER, CAPTAIN EDWARD HASTINGS, TO LEAD IT.

WITH CHILD, VIVIAN KNOWS THAT HER HUSBAND WILL REPUDIATE HER—OR WORSE—ONCE HE DISCOVERS SHE IS PREGNANT.

SO SHE CONVINCES DR LIVESEY TO HELP HER CONTACT PIRATE LONG JOHN SILVER AND HIS BROTHERS OF THE COAST…

VIVIAN'S PLAN SUCCEEDS: THE "NEPTUNE" SAILS AWAY WITH PART OF THE CREW SUPPOSEDLY AT HER COMMAND TO GET HER OUT OF THE TIGHT SPOT IN WHICH HER HUSBAND HAS PUT HER.

WHAT SHE DOESN'T KNOW IS THAT LONG JOHN SILVER IS IN A VERY DELICATE SITUATION, TOO. SUBJECT TO GRAVE BOUTS OF MALARIA, HE DOESN'T HAVE ENOUGH MEN TO TAKE THE SHIP. AND ONE OF THEM, PARIS, HAS EVEN FORCED HIM TO HIRE HIS YOUNG PROTÉGÉ, JACK O'KIEF. EVEN WORSE: LADY VIVIAN'S OWN MAID IS ABOUT TO BETRAY TO THE CAPTAIN THE BLOOD PACT SIGNED BETWEEN THE LADY AND THE PIRATES…

Original title: Long John Silver II – Neptune
Original edition: © Dargaud Paris, 2008 by Dorison & Lauffray
www.dargaud.com  -  All rights reserved
English translation: © 2011 Cinebook Ltd
Translator: Jerome Saincantin
Lettering and text layout: Imadjinn
Printed in Spain by Just Colour Graphic
This edition first published in Great Britain in 2011 by
Cinebook Ltd  -  56 Beech Avenue
Canterbury, Kent  -  CT4 7TA
www.cinebook.com
A CIP catalogue record for this book
is available from the British Library
ISBN 978-1-84918-072-6

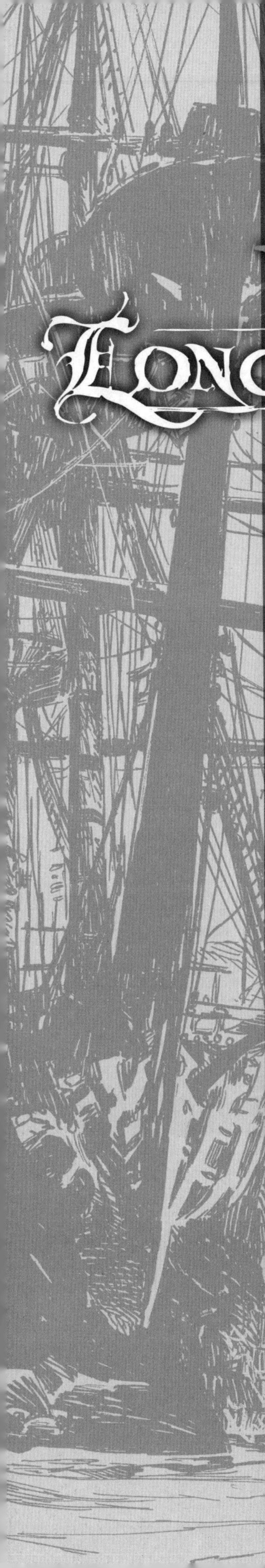

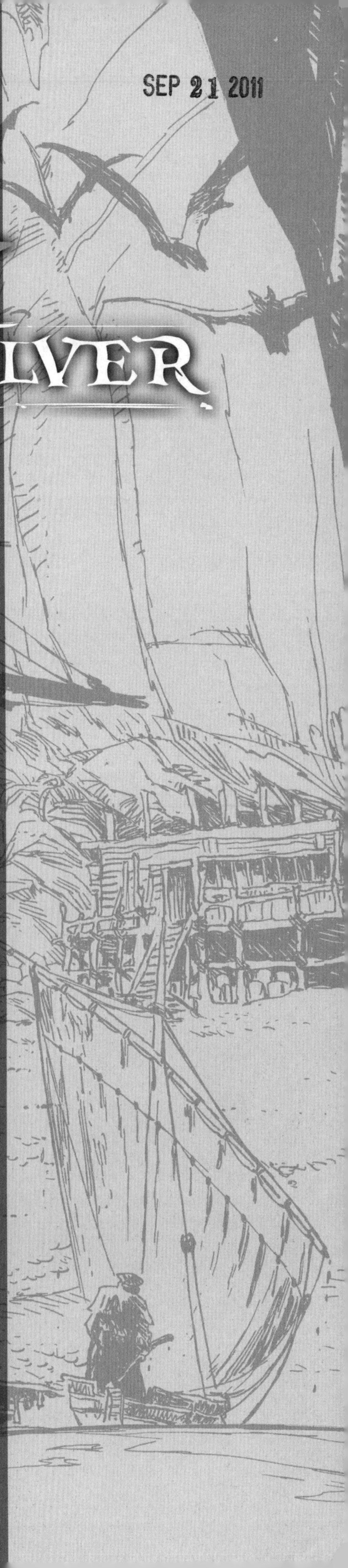



# LONG JOHN SILVER

II - NEPTUNE

XAVIER
DORISON

MATHIEU
LAUFFRAY

9th CINEBOOK
The 9th Art Publisher

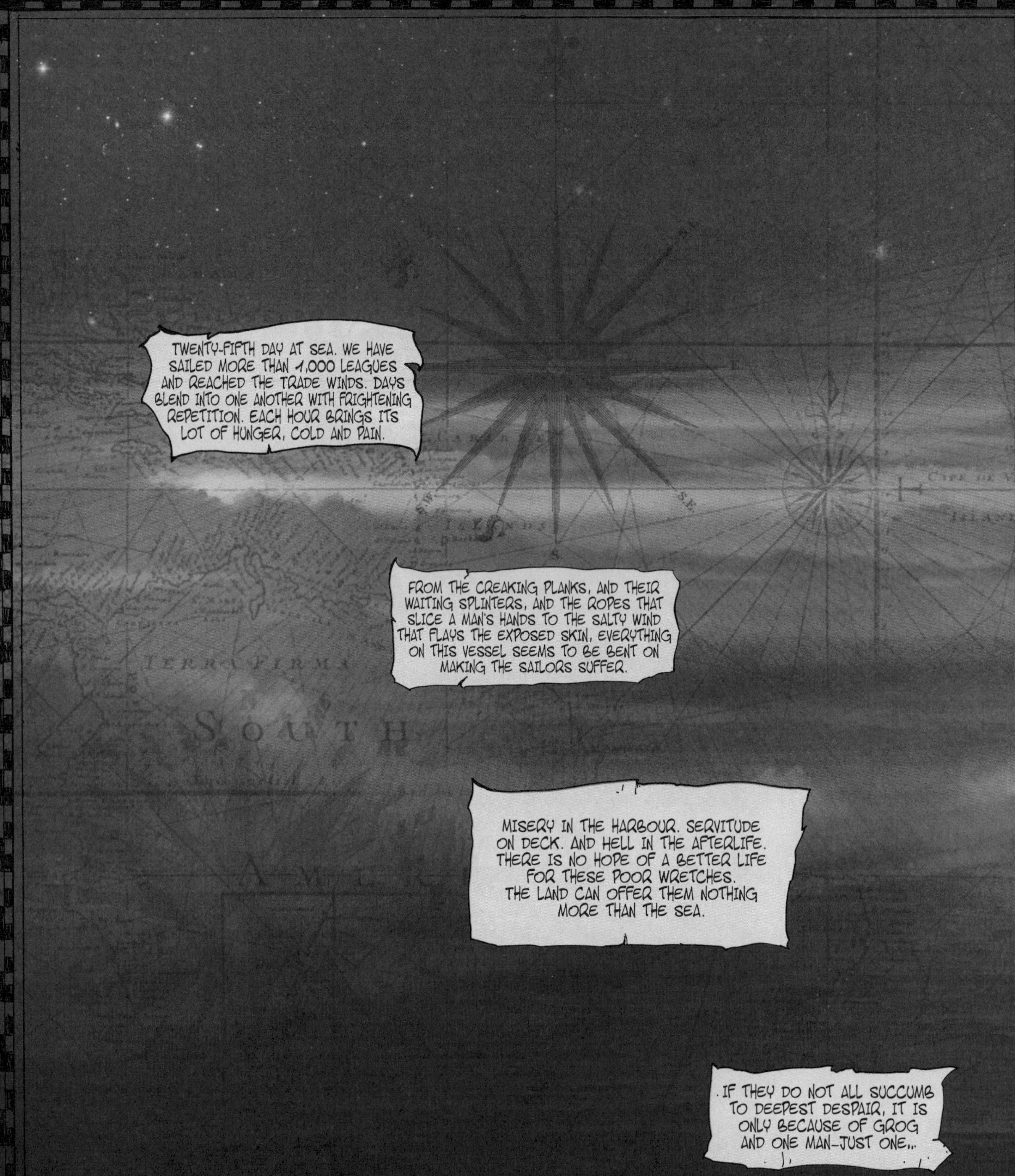
TWENTY-FIFTH DAY AT SEA. WE HAVE SAILED MORE THAN 1,000 LEAGUES AND REACHED THE TRADE WINDS. DAYS BLEND INTO ONE ANOTHER WITH FRIGHTENING REPETITION. EACH HOUR BRINGS ITS LOT OF HUNGER, COLD AND PAIN.
FROM THE CREAKING PLANKS, AND THEIR WAITING SPLINTERS, AND THE ROPES THAT SLICE A MAN'S HANDS TO THE SALTY WIND THAT FLAYS THE EXPOSED SKIN, EVERYTHING ON THIS VESSEL SEEMS TO BE BENT ON MAKING THE SAILORS SUFFER.
TERRA FIRMA
SOUTH
MISERY IN THE HARBOUR. SERVITUDE ON DECK. AND HELL IN THE AFTERLIFE. THERE IS NO HOPE OF A BETTER LIFE FOR THESE POOR WRETCHES. THE LAND CAN OFFER THEM NOTHING MORE THAN THE SEA.
IF THEY DO NOT ALL SUCCUMB TO DEEPEST DESPAIR, IT IS ONLY BECAUSE OF GROG AND ONE MAN–JUST ONE...

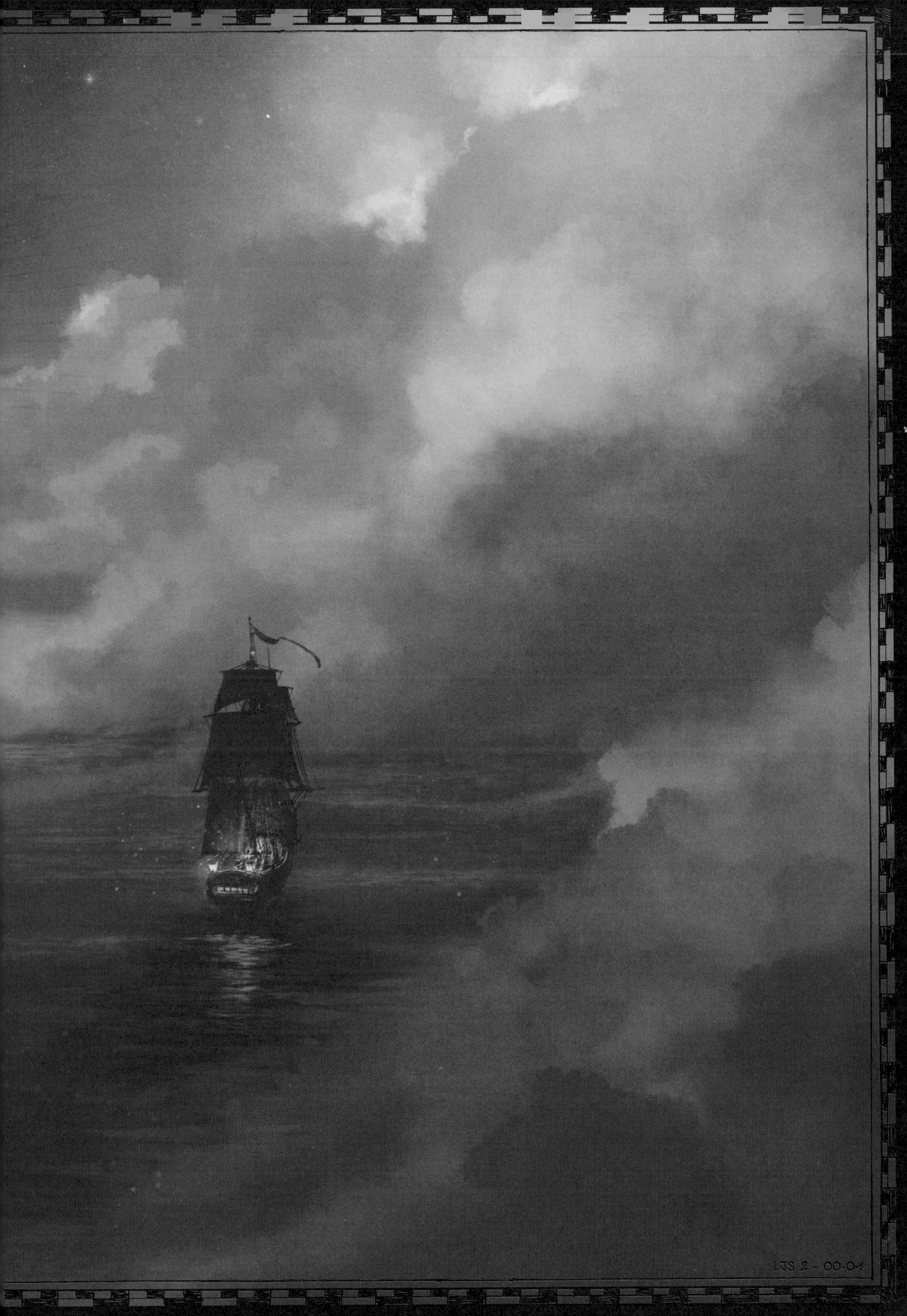
LJS 2 - 00-01

... AND THEN, CAPTAIN FLINT ASKS ME IF I'M A PIRATE...
SO I TELLS HIM: "NO!"

"I'M A COOK!"

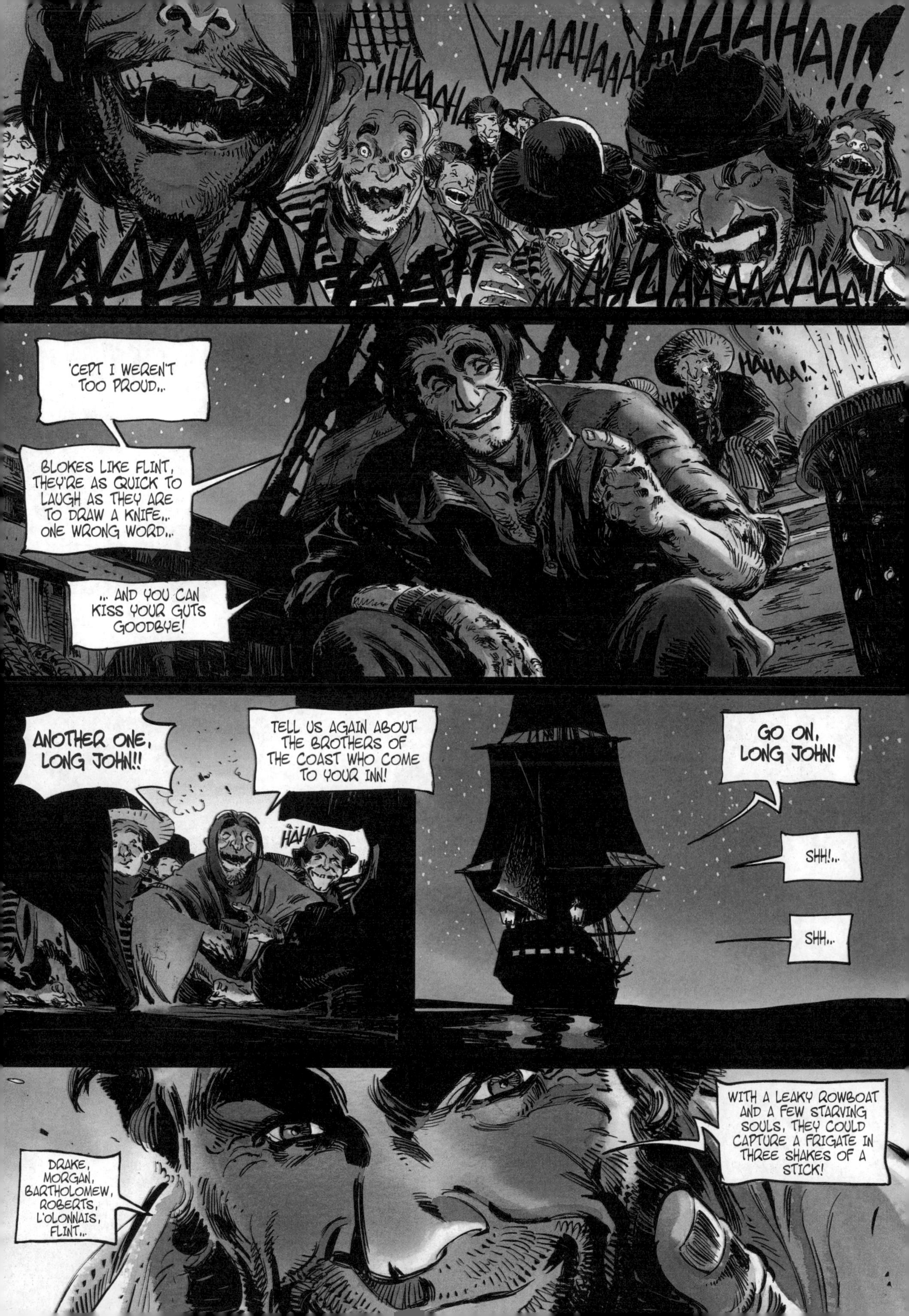
HAAAHAAAA HAAHHA!!
HAAAHAA
HAAAAAHAAA!!
HAAAAAAAAAAA!!
'CEPT I WEREN'T TOO PROUD...
BLOKES LIKE FLINT, THEY'RE AS QUICK TO LAUGH AS THEY ARE TO DRAW A KNIFE... ONE WRONG WORD...
... AND YOU CAN KISS YOUR GUTS GOODBYE!
HAHAA!!
ANOTHER ONE, LONG JOHN!!
TELL US AGAIN ABOUT THE BROTHERS OF THE COAST WHO COME TO YOUR INN!
HAHA
GO ON, LONG JOHN!
SHH!...
SHH...
DRAKE, MORGAN, BARTHOLOMEW, ROBERTS, L'OLONNAIS, FLINT...
WITH A LEAKY ROWBOAT AND A FEW STARVING SOULS, THEY COULD CAPTURE A FRIGATE IN THREE SHAKES OF A STICK!

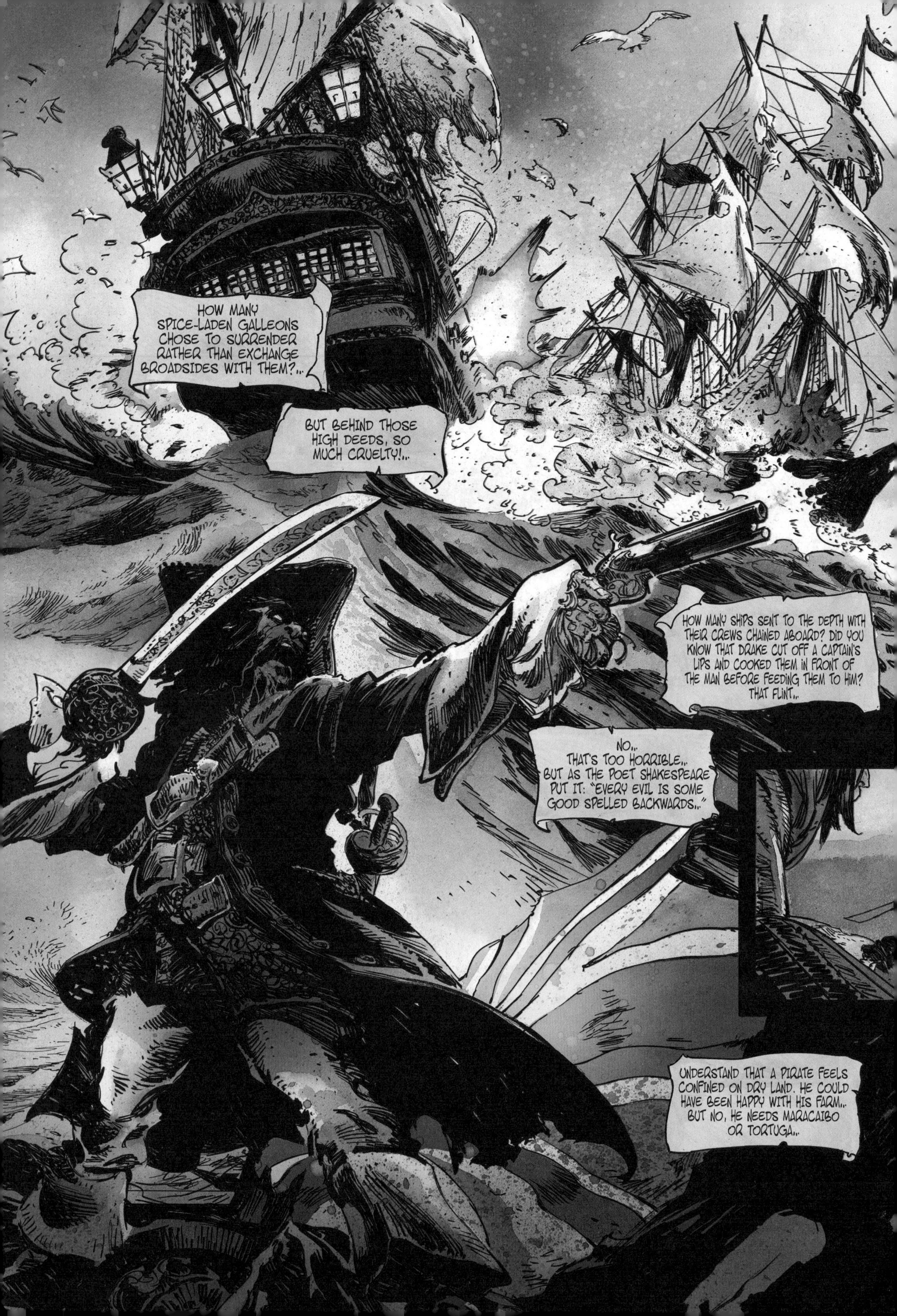
HOW MANY SPICE-LADEN GALLEONS CHOSE TO SURRENDER RATHER THAN EXCHANGE BROADSIDES WITH THEM?..
BUT BEHIND THOSE HIGH DEEDS, SO MUCH CRUELTY!..
HOW MANY SHIPS SENT TO THE DEPTH WITH THEIR CREWS CHAINED ABOARD? DID YOU KNOW THAT DRAKE CUT OFF A CAPTAIN'S LIPS AND COOKED THEM IN FRONT OF THE MAN BEFORE FEEDING THEM TO HIM? THAT FLINT..
NO.. THAT'S TOO HORRIBLE.. BUT AS THE POET SHAKESPEARE PUT IT: "EVERY EVIL IS SOME GOOD SPELLED BACKWARDS.."
UNDERSTAND THAT A PIRATE FEELS CONFINED ON DRY LAND. HE COULD HAVE BEEN HAPPY WITH HIS FARM.. BUT NO, HE NEEDS MARACAIBO OR TORTUGA..

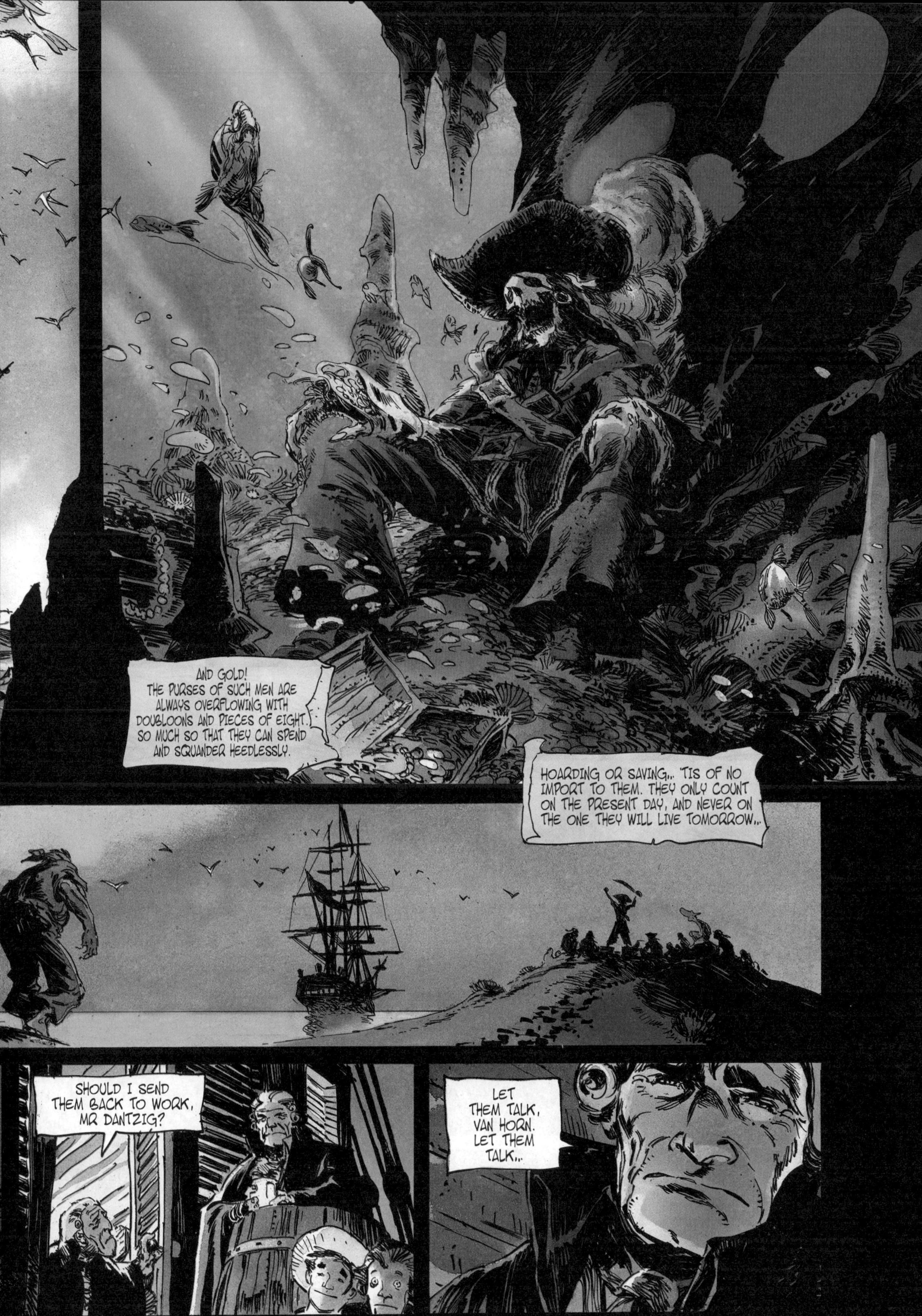
AND GOLD! THE PURSES OF SUCH MEN ARE ALWAYS OVERFLOWING WITH DOUBLOONS AND PIECES OF EIGHT. SO MUCH SO THAT THEY CAN SPEND AND SQUANDER HEEDLESSLY.
HOARDING OR SAVING... 'TIS OF NO IMPORT TO THEM. THEY ONLY COUNT ON THE PRESENT DAY, AND NEVER ON THE ONE THEY WILL LIVE TOMORROW...
SHOULD I SEND THEM BACK TO WORK, MR DANTZIG?
LET THEM TALK, VAN HORN. LET THEM TALK...

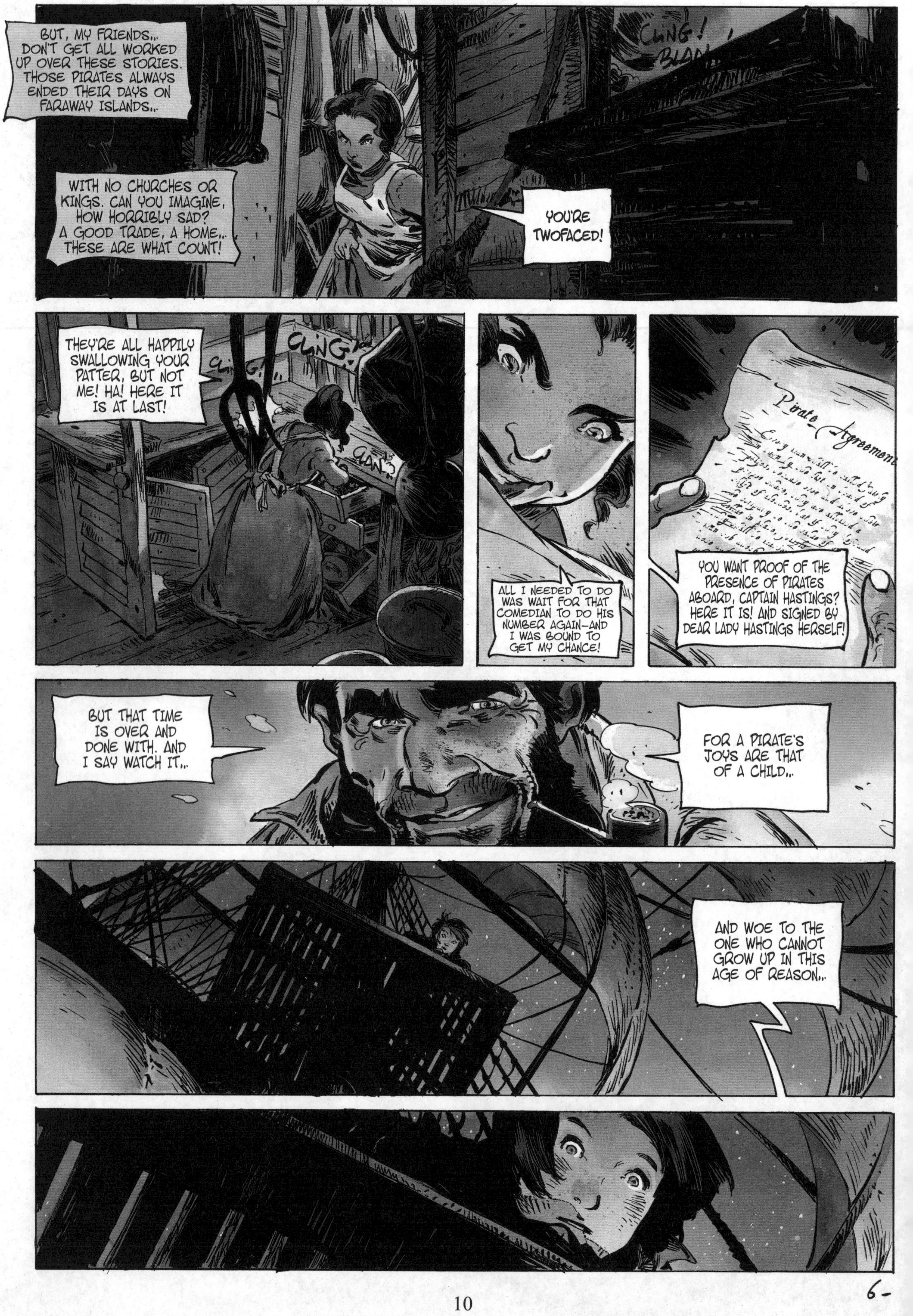
BUT, MY FRIENDS... DON'T GET ALL WORKED UP OVER THESE STORIES. THOSE PIRATES ALWAYS ENDED THEIR DAYS ON FARAWAY ISLANDS...
CLING!
WITH NO CHURCHES OR KINGS. CAN YOU IMAGINE, HOW HORRIBLY SAD? A GOOD TRADE, A HOME... THESE ARE WHAT COUNT!
YOU'RE TWOFACED!
THEY'RE ALL HAPPILY SWALLOWING YOUR PATTER, BUT NOT ME! HA! HERE IT IS AT LAST!
CLING!
ALL I NEEDED TO DO WAS WAIT FOR THAT COMEDIAN TO DO HIS NUMBER AGAIN—AND I WAS BOUND TO GET MY CHANCE!
Pirate Agreement
YOU WANT PROOF OF THE PRESENCE OF PIRATES ABOARD, CAPTAIN HASTINGS? HERE IT IS! AND SIGNED BY DEAR LADY HASTINGS HERSELF!
BUT THAT TIME IS OVER AND DONE WITH. AND I SAY WATCH IT...
FOR A PIRATE'S JOYS ARE THAT OF A CHILD...
AND WOE TO THE ONE WHO CANNOT GROW UP IN THIS AGE OF REASON...



6-

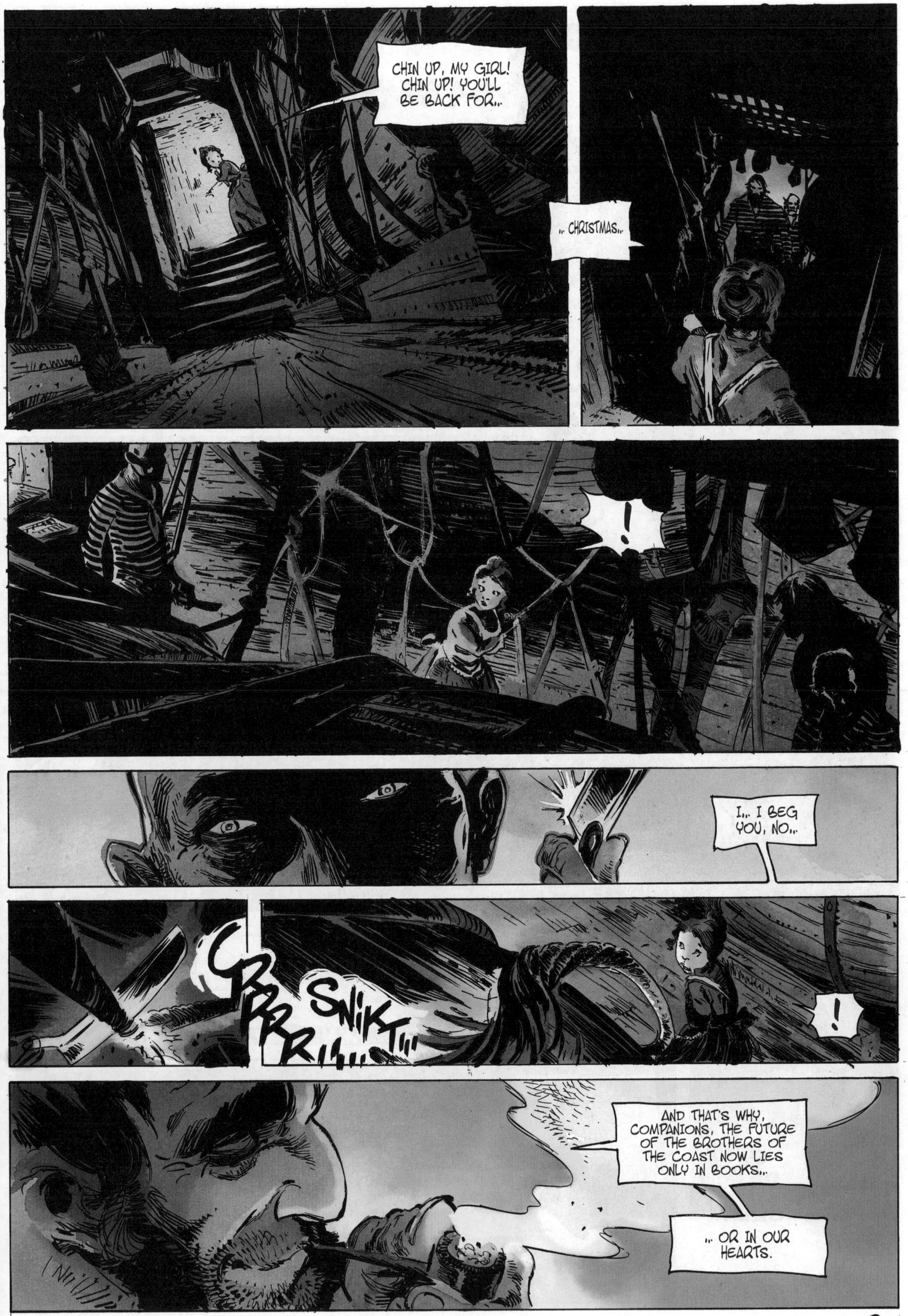
CHIN UP, MY GIRL! CHIN UP! YOU'LL BE BACK FOR..
.. CHRISTMAS..
!
I.. I BEG YOU, NO..
CRRRR!...
SNIKT!!!
!
AND THAT'S WHY, COMPANIONS, THE FUTURE OF THE BROTHERS OF THE COAST NOW LIES ONLY IN BOOKS..
.. OR IN OUR HEARTS.

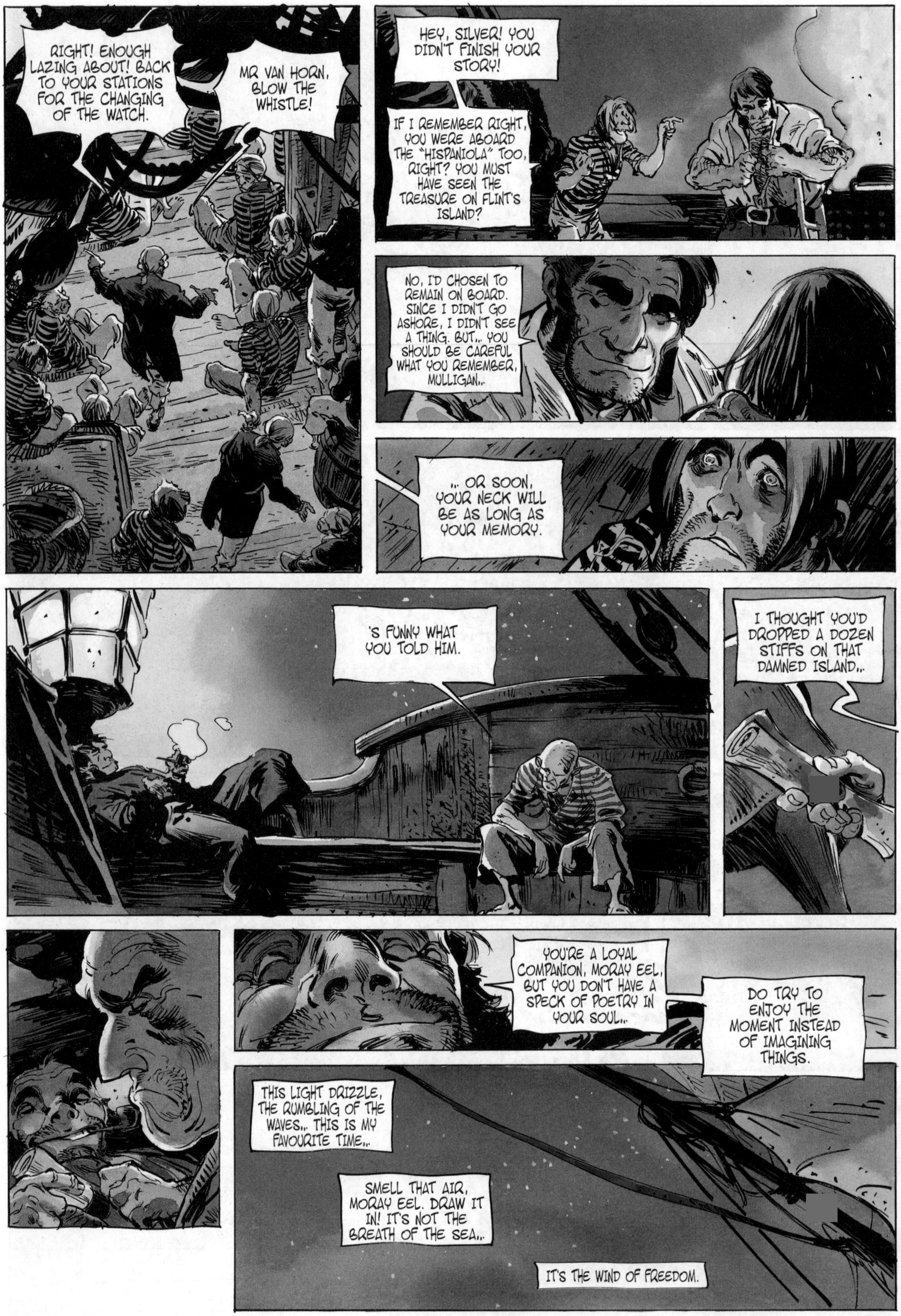
RIGHT! ENOUGH LAZING ABOUT! BACK TO YOUR STATIONS FOR THE CHANGING OF THE WATCH.
MR VAN HORN, BLOW THE WHISTLE!
HEY, SILVER! YOU DIDN'T FINISH YOUR STORY!
IF I REMEMBER RIGHT, YOU WERE ABOARD THE "HISPANIOLA" TOO, RIGHT? YOU MUST HAVE SEEN THE TREASURE ON FLINT'S ISLAND?
NO, I'D CHOSEN TO REMAIN ON BOARD. SINCE I DIDN'T GO ASHORE, I DIDN'T SEE A THING. BUT... YOU SHOULD BE CAREFUL WHAT YOU REMEMBER, MULLIGAN...
... OR SOON, YOUR NECK WILL BE AS LONG AS YOUR MEMORY.
'S FUNNY WHAT YOU TOLD HIM.
I THOUGHT YOU'D DROPPED A DOZEN STIFFS ON THAT DAMNED ISLAND...
YOU'RE A LOYAL COMPANION, MORAY EEL, BUT YOU DON'T HAVE A SPECK OF POETRY IN YOUR SOUL...
DO TRY TO ENJOY THE MOMENT INSTEAD OF IMAGINING THINGS.
THIS LIGHT DRIZZLE, THE RUMBLING OF THE WAVES... THIS IS MY FAVOURITE TIME...
SMELL THAT AIR, MORAY EEL. DRAW IT IN! IT'S NOT THE BREATH OF THE SEA...
IT'S THE WIND OF FREEDOM.

8-

WE ARE LEAVING THE TRADE WINDS AND HAVE PASSED THE FIFTEENTH PARALLEL. IN TWO WEEKS WE WILL REACH THE GULF OF PARIA.

IN FAITH, I MUST SAY MY NAVIGATION WAS RATHER GOOD.

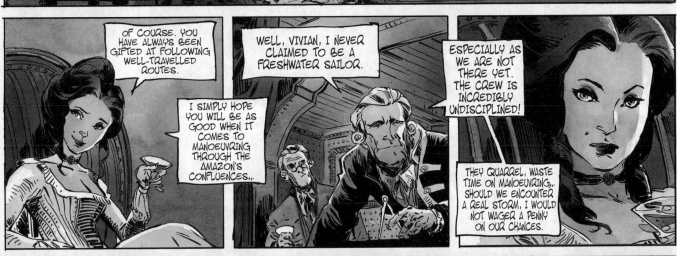

OF COURSE. YOU HAVE ALWAYS BEEN GIFTED AT FOLLOWING WELL-TRAVELLED ROUTES.

I SIMPLY HOPE YOU WILL BE AS GOOD WHEN IT COMES TO MANOEUVRING THROUGH THE AMAZON'S CONFLUENCES...

WELL, VIVIAN, I NEVER CLAIMED TO BE A FRESHWATER SAILOR.

ESPECIALLY AS WE ARE NOT THERE YET. THE CREW IS INCREDIBLY UNDISCIPLINED!

THEY QUARREL, WASTE TIME ON MANOEUVRING... SHOULD WE ENCOUNTER A REAL STORM, I WOULD NOT WAGER A PENNY ON OUR CHANCES.

WE HAVE BEEN LUCKY SO FAR. IT WILL NOT LAST LONG.

SOON, BYRON'S MAP AND MOC'S GUIDANCE WILL BE THE ONLY DIRECTIONS AVAILABLE TO US... LET US HOPE THAT NATIVE KNOWS WHAT HE IS ABOUT.

CAPTAIN!

IT'S THE SERVANT GIRL! THERE'S BEEN AN ACCIDENT!

!

9—

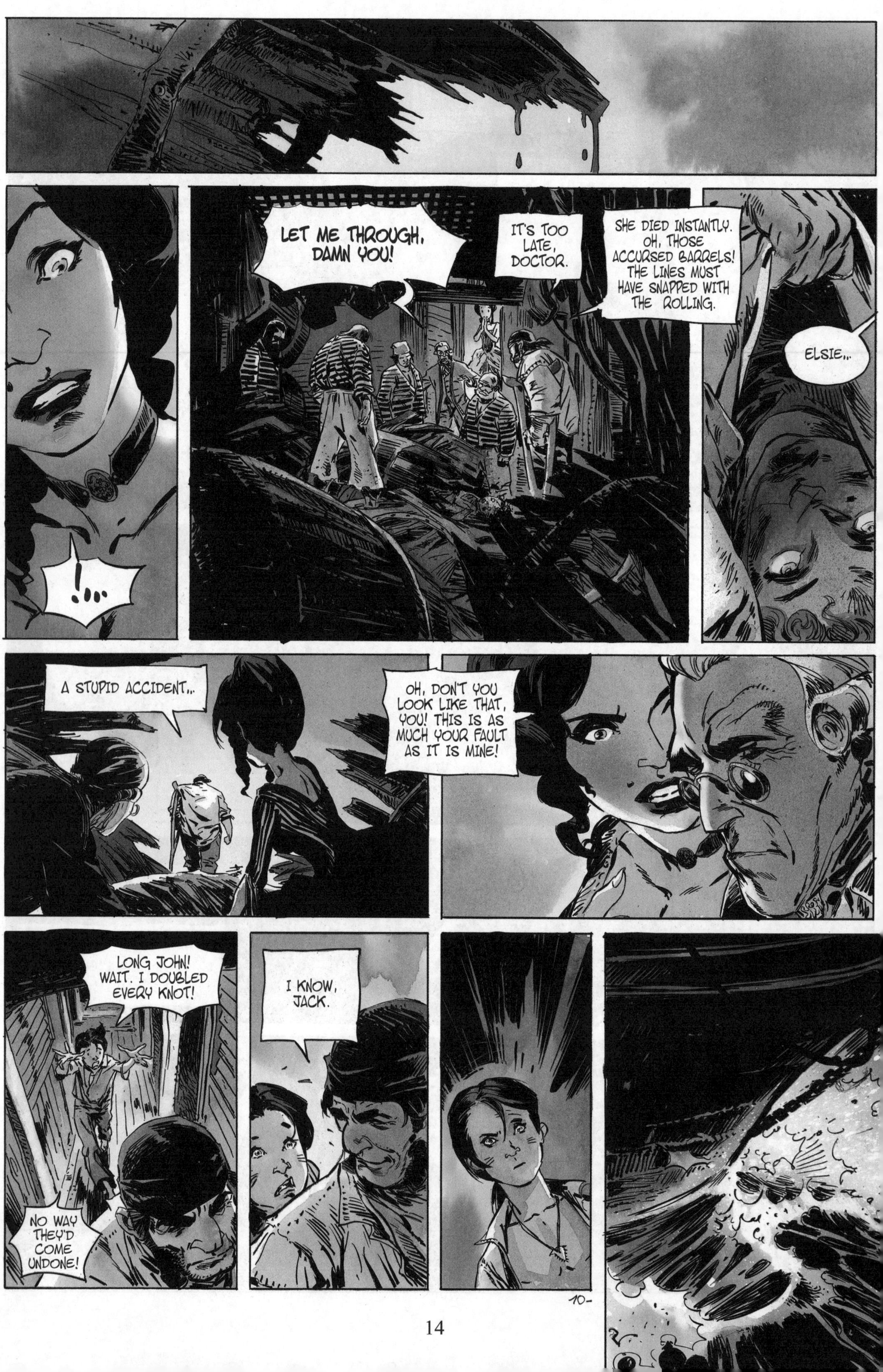

!...
LET ME THROUGH, DAMN YOU!
IT'S TOO LATE, DOCTOR.
SHE DIED INSTANTLY. OH, THOSE ACCURSED BARRELS! THE LINES MUST HAVE SNAPPED WITH THE ROLLING.
ELSIE...
A STUPID ACCIDENT...
OH, DON'T YOU LOOK LIKE THAT, YOU! THIS IS AS MUCH YOUR FAULT AS IT IS MINE!
LONG JOHN! WAIT. I DOUBLED EVERY KNOT!
NO WAY THEY'D COME UNDONE!
I KNOW, JACK.
10-

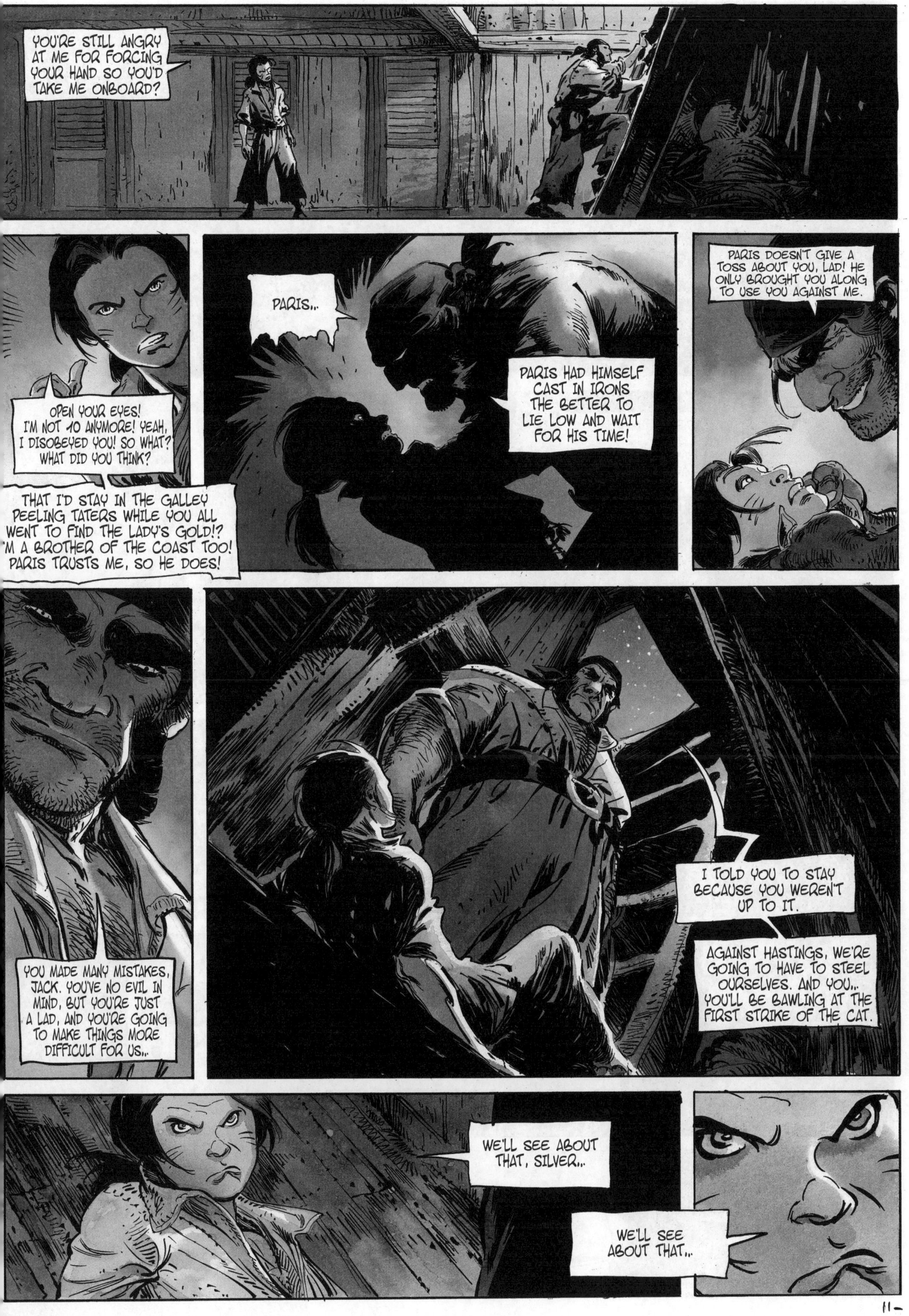
YOU'RE STILL ANGRY AT ME FOR FORCING YOUR HAND SO YOU'D TAKE ME ONBOARD?
OPEN YOUR EYES! I'M NOT 10 ANYMORE! YEAH, I DISOBEYED YOU! SO WHAT? WHAT DID YOU THINK?
THAT I'D STAY IN THE GALLEY PEELING TATERS WHILE YOU ALL WENT TO FIND THE LADY'S GOLD!? I'M A BROTHER OF THE COAST TOO! PARIS TRUSTS ME, SO HE DOES!
PARIS...
PARIS HAD HIMSELF CAST IN IRONS THE BETTER TO LIE LOW AND WAIT FOR HIS TIME!
PARIS DOESN'T GIVE A TOSS ABOUT YOU, LAD! HE ONLY BROUGHT YOU ALONG TO USE YOU AGAINST ME.
YOU MADE MANY MISTAKES, JACK. YOU'VE NO EVIL IN MIND, BUT YOU'RE JUST A LAD, AND YOU'RE GOING TO MAKE THINGS MORE DIFFICULT FOR US...
I TOLD YOU TO STAY BECAUSE YOU WEREN'T UP TO IT.
AGAINST HASTINGS, WE'RE GOING TO HAVE TO STEEL OURSELVES. AND YOU... YOU'LL BE BAWLING AT THE FIRST STRIKE OF THE CAT.
WE'LL SEE ABOUT THAT, SILVER...
WE'LL SEE ABOUT THAT...
11

DOCTOR LIVESEY AND LADY VIVIAN DECLINED TO JOIN ME FOR BRANDY.

NO DOUBT THE REGRETTABLE LOSS OF MISS DODWOOD HAS SOMETHING TO DO WITH THIS. A RATHER UNPLEASANT SIGHT, IN TRUTH.

WHAT DO YOU THINK, MR SILVER?

I'M SURE A MAN SO IN TUNE WITH THE MEN MUST HAVE AN OPINION ON THAT POINT.

MAY THAT POOR WOMAN'S SOUL REST IN PEACE. THE SEA WASN'T MADE FOR HER. IT WAS THE SEA THAT TOOK HER, AFTER ALL.

INDEED, INDEED. UNLESS IT WAS YOUR COOKING, SILVER.

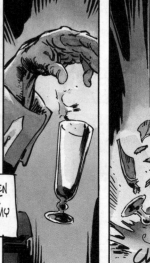

TOO HEAVY, TOO STRONG. AN EXCESS OF SPICES AND SAUCES. YOUR BAROQUE NATURE LEADS YOU ASTRAY, AND IT IRRITATES ME.

I WOULD EVEN SAY THAT IT WEIGHS ON MY STOMACH.

CLING!!

12—

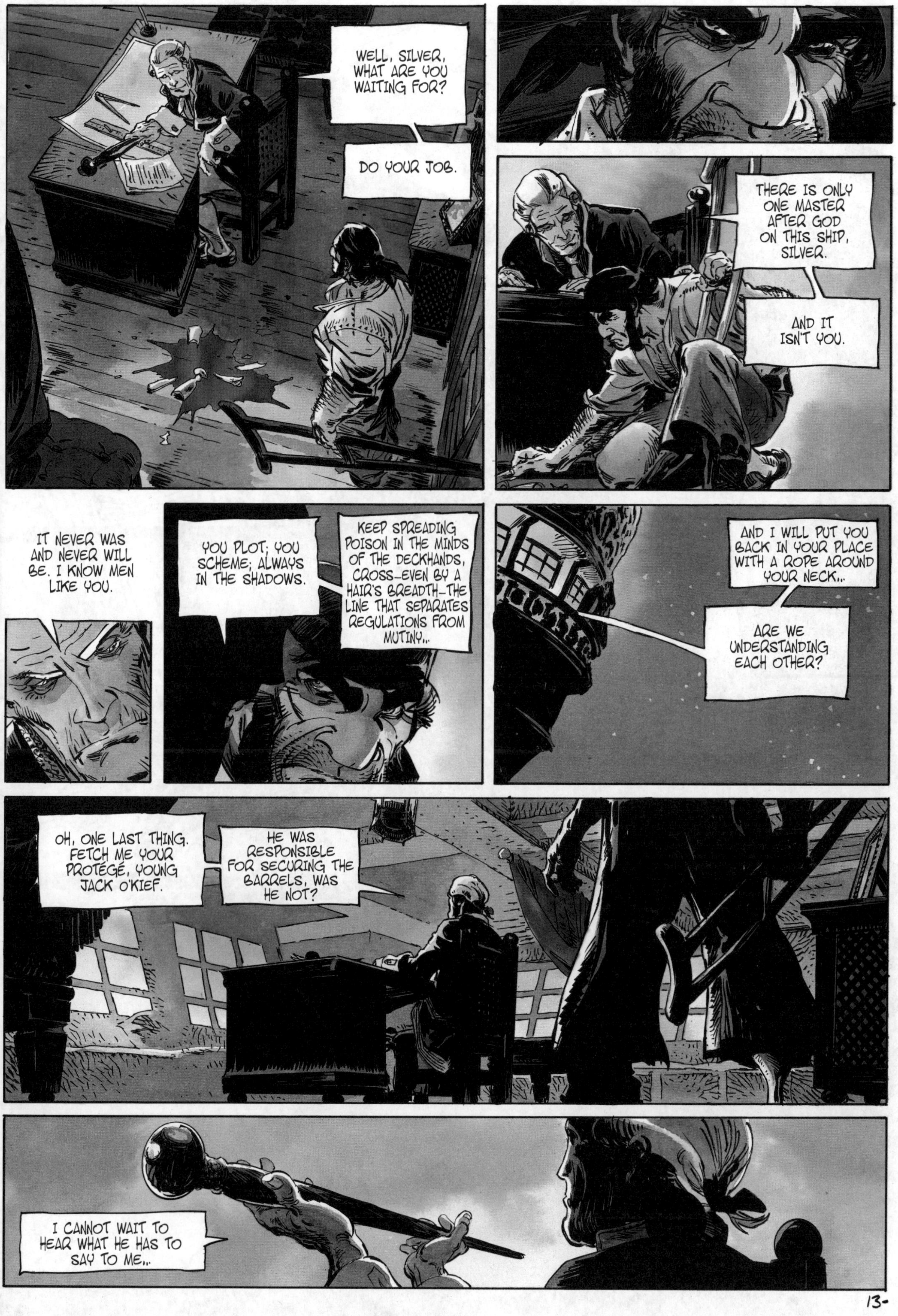
WELL, SILVER, WHAT ARE YOU WAITING FOR?
DO YOUR JOB.
THERE IS ONLY ONE MASTER AFTER GOD ON THIS SHIP, SILVER.
AND IT ISN'T YOU.
IT NEVER WAS AND NEVER WILL BE. I KNOW MEN LIKE YOU.
YOU PLOT; YOU SCHEME; ALWAYS IN THE SHADOWS.
KEEP SPREADING POISON IN THE MINDS OF THE DECKHANDS, CROSS–EVEN BY A HAIR'S BREADTH–THE LINE THAT SEPARATES REGULATIONS FROM MUTINY...
AND I WILL PUT YOU BACK IN YOUR PLACE WITH A ROPE AROUND YOUR NECK...
ARE WE UNDERSTANDING EACH OTHER?
OH, ONE LAST THING. FETCH ME YOUR PROTÉGÉ, YOUNG JACK O'KIEF.
HE WAS RESPONSIBLE FOR SECURING THE BARRELS, WAS HE NOT?
I CANNOT WAIT TO HEAR WHAT HE HAS TO SAY TO ME...
13-

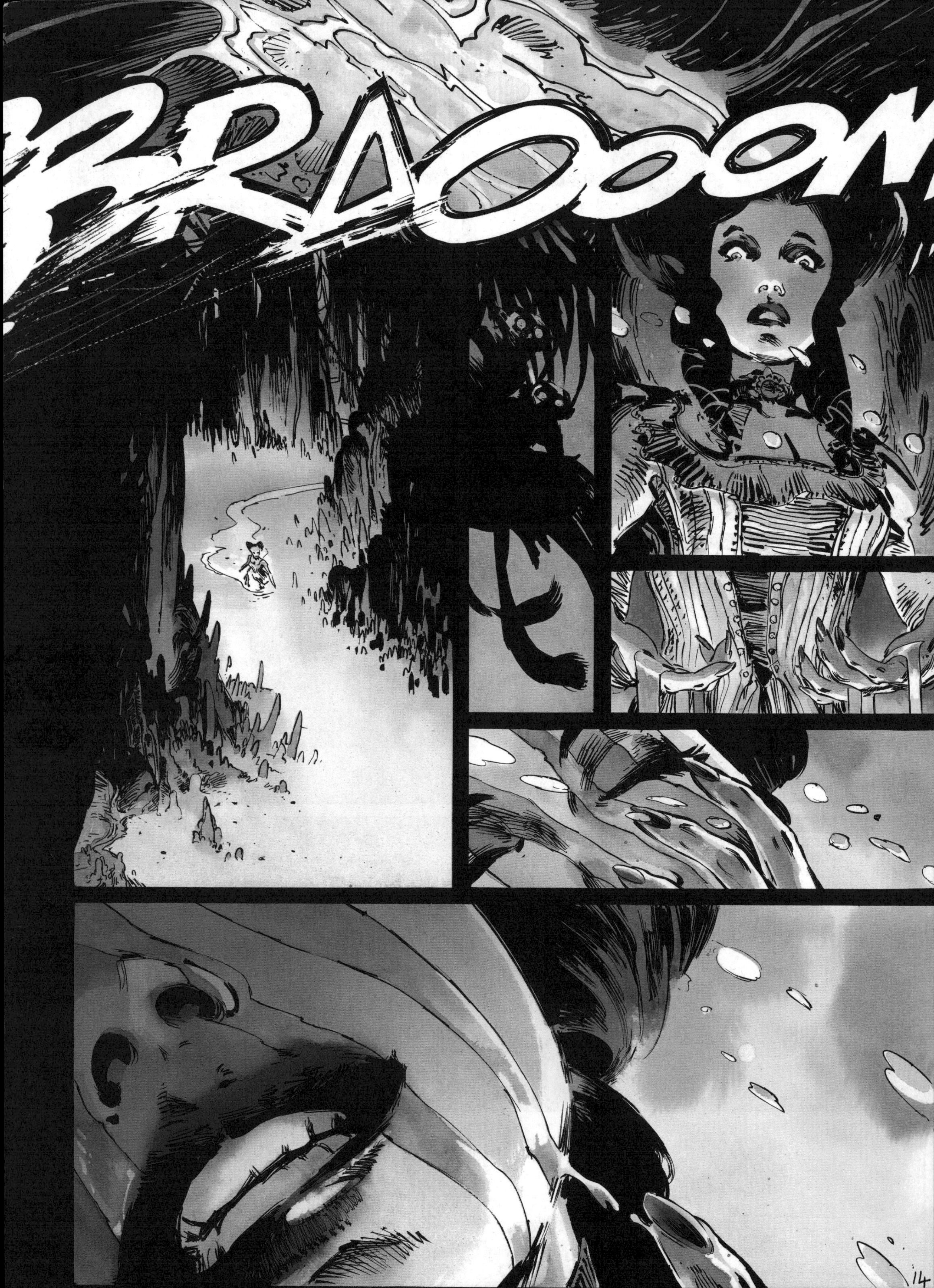
BRAOOOOM

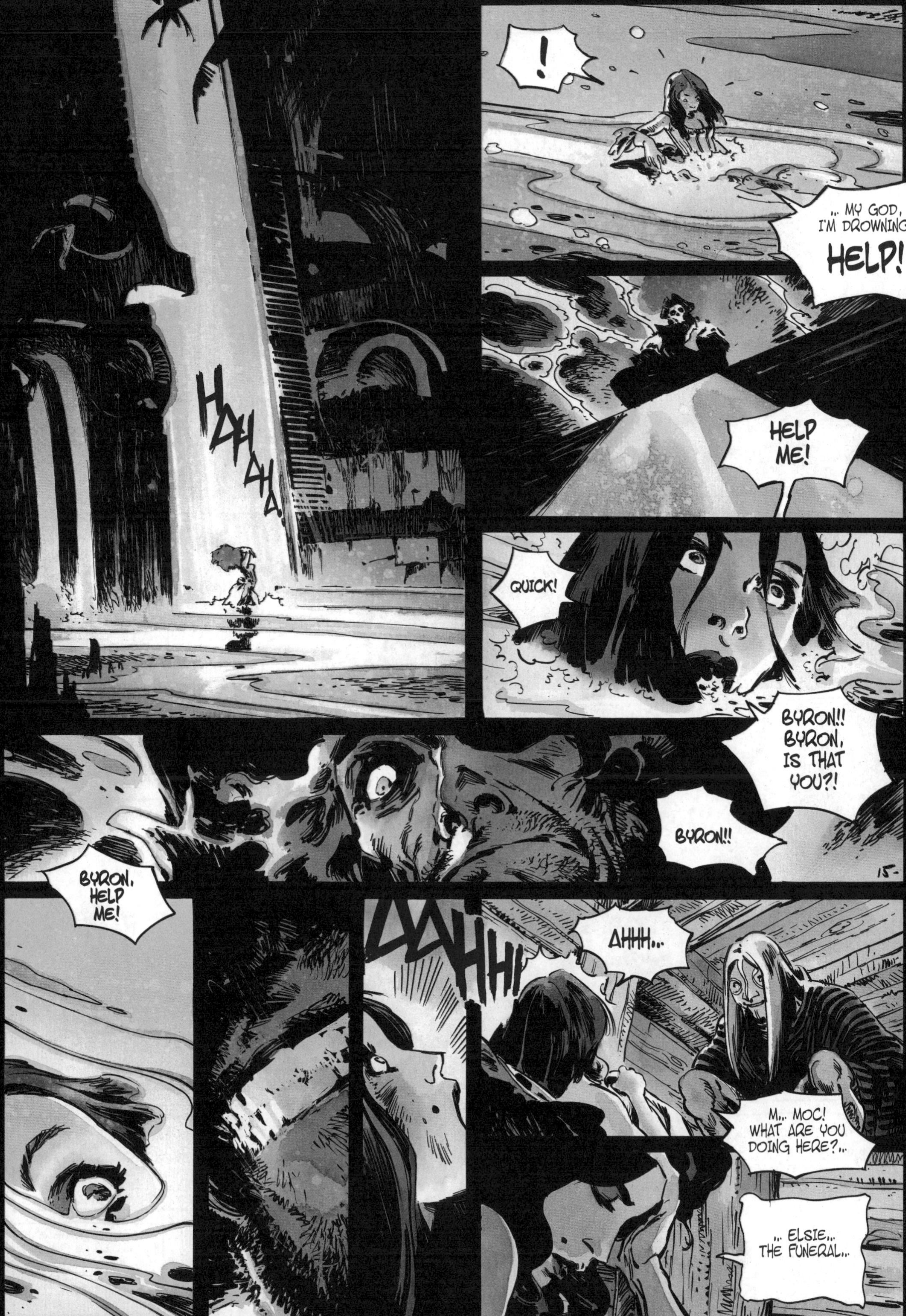
HAHAHA!
!
.. MY GOD, I'M DROWNING!
HELP!
HELP ME!
QUICK!
BYRON!! BYRON, IS THAT YOU?!
BYRON!!
15-
BYRON, HELP ME!
AAAHH!
AHHH...
M.. MOC! WHAT ARE YOU DOING HERE?..
.. ELSIE.. THE FUNERAL..

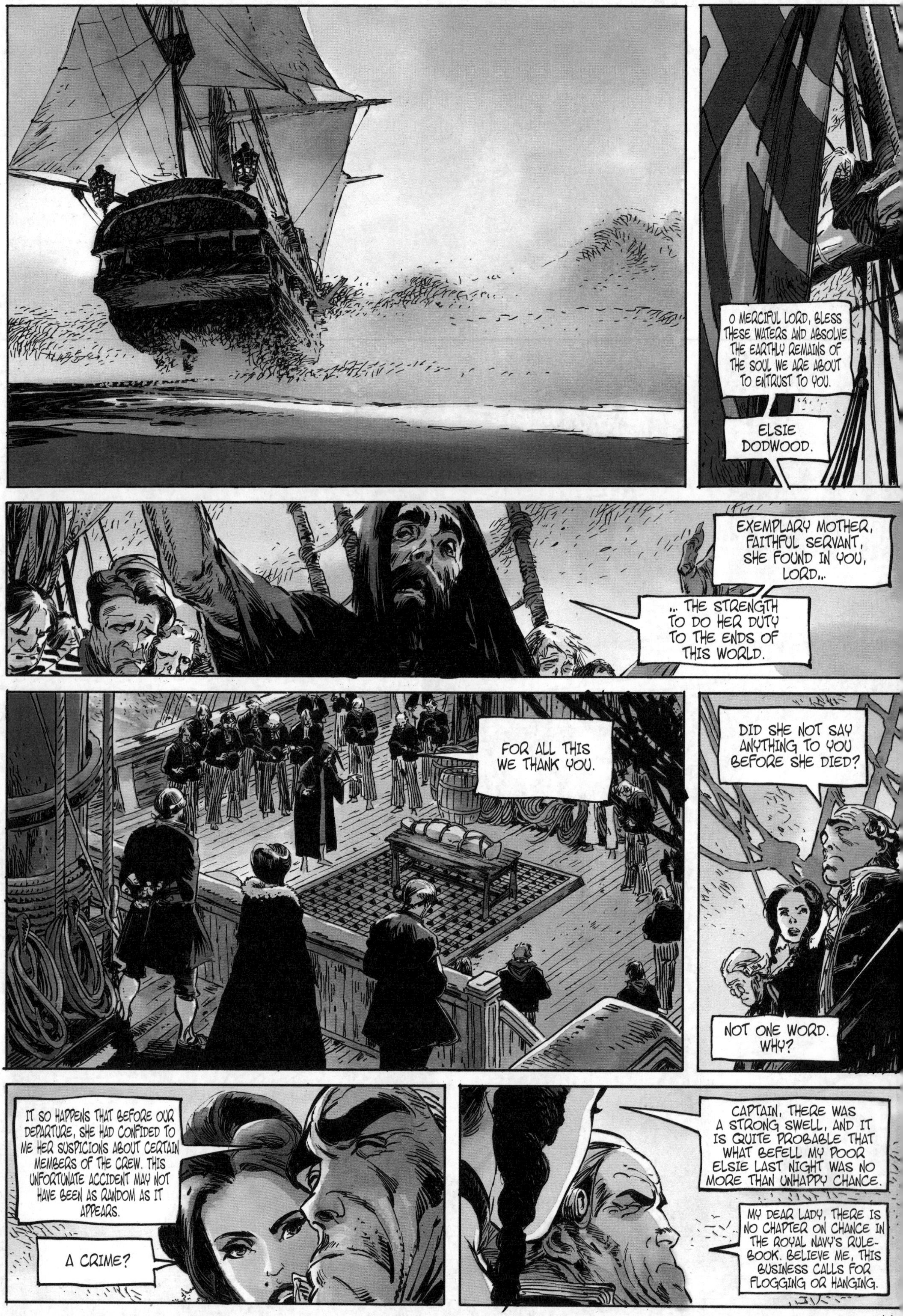
O MERCIFUL LORD, BLESS THESE WATERS AND ABSOLVE THE EARTHLY REMAINS OF THE SOUL WE ARE ABOUT TO ENTRUST TO YOU.
ELSIE DODWOOD.
EXEMPLARY MOTHER, FAITHFUL SERVANT, SHE FOUND IN YOU, LORD...
... THE STRENGTH TO DO HER DUTY TO THE ENDS OF THIS WORLD.
FOR ALL THIS WE THANK YOU.
DID SHE NOT SAY ANYTHING TO YOU BEFORE SHE DIED?
NOT ONE WORD. WHY?
IT SO HAPPENS THAT BEFORE OUR DEPARTURE, SHE HAD CONFIDED TO ME HER SUSPICIONS ABOUT CERTAIN MEMBERS OF THE CREW. THIS UNFORTUNATE ACCIDENT MAY NOT HAVE BEEN AS RANDOM AS IT APPEARS.
A CRIME?
CAPTAIN, THERE WAS A STRONG SWELL, AND IT IS QUITE PROBABLE THAT WHAT BEFELL MY POOR ELSIE LAST NIGHT WAS NO MORE THAN UNHAPPY CHANCE.
MY DEAR LADY, THERE IS NO CHAPTER ON CHANCE IN THE ROYAL NAVY'S RULE-BOOK. BELIEVE ME, THIS BUSINESS CALLS FOR FLOGGING OR HANGING.
16

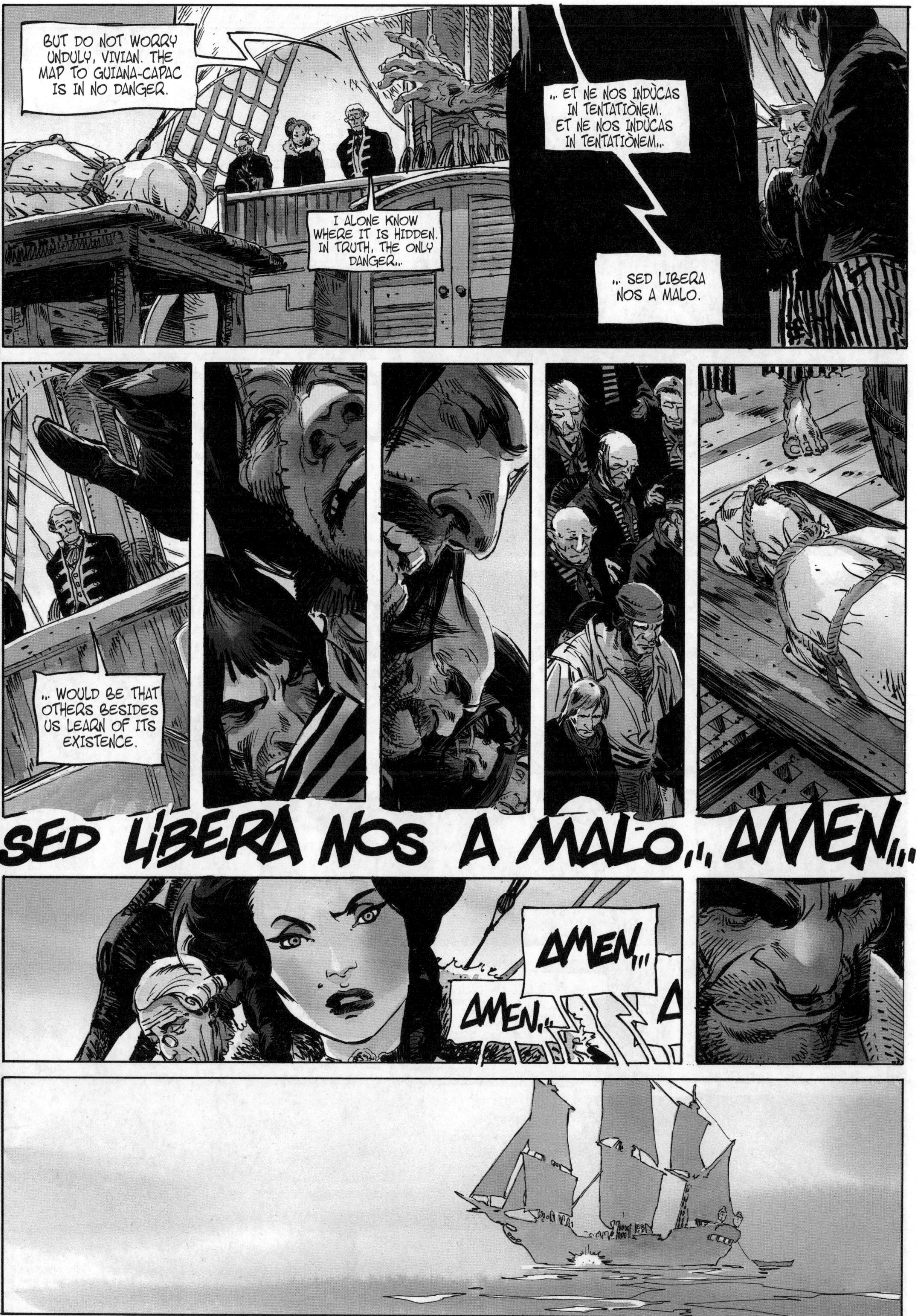
BUT DO NOT WORRY UNDULY, VIVIAN. THE MAP TO GUIANA-CAPAC IS IN NO DANGER.
I ALONE KNOW WHERE IT IS HIDDEN. IN TRUTH, THE ONLY DANGER...
... ET NE NOS INDÙCAS IN TENTATIÒNEM. ET NE NOS INDÙCAS IN TENTATIÒNEM...
... SED LIBERA NOS A MALO.
... WOULD BE THAT OTHERS BESIDES US LEARN OF ITS EXISTENCE.
SED LIBERA NOS A MALO... AMEN...
AMEN...
AMEN...
A

17

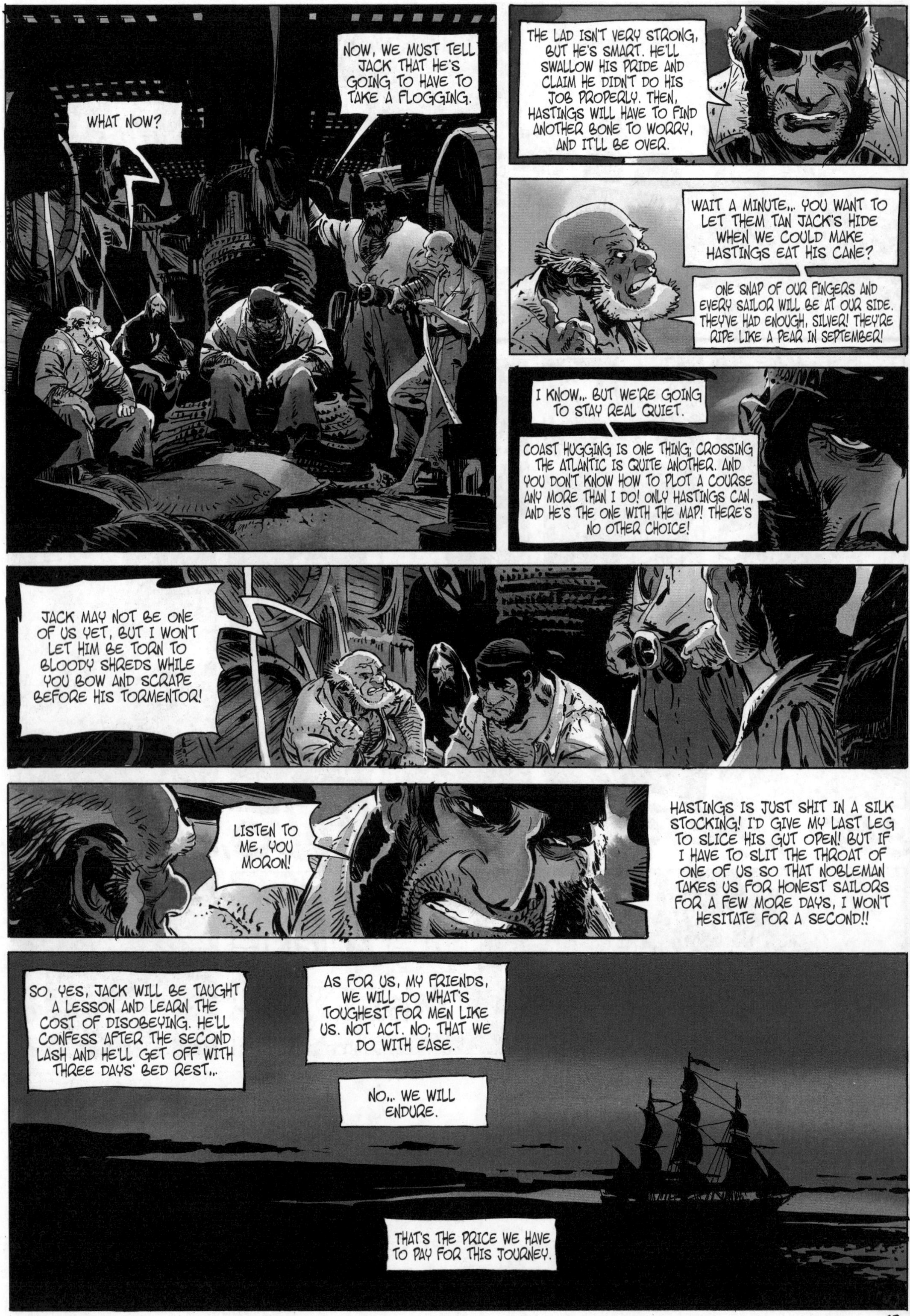
NOW, WE MUST TELL JACK THAT HE'S GOING TO HAVE TO TAKE A FLOGGING.
WHAT NOW?
THE LAD ISN'T VERY STRONG, BUT HE'S SMART. HE'LL SWALLOW HIS PRIDE AND CLAIM HE DIDN'T DO HIS JOB PROPERLY. THEN, HASTINGS WILL HAVE TO FIND ANOTHER BONE TO WORRY, AND IT'LL BE OVER.
WAIT A MINUTE... YOU WANT TO LET THEM TAN JACK'S HIDE WHEN WE COULD MAKE HASTINGS EAT HIS CANE?
ONE SNAP OF OUR FINGERS AND EVERY SAILOR WILL BE AT OUR SIDE. THEY'VE HAD ENOUGH, SILVER! THEY'RE RIPE LIKE A PEAR IN SEPTEMBER!
I KNOW... BUT WE'RE GOING TO STAY REAL QUIET.
COAST HUGGING IS ONE THING; CROSSING THE ATLANTIC IS QUITE ANOTHER. AND YOU DON'T KNOW HOW TO PLOT A COURSE ANY MORE THAN I DO! ONLY HASTINGS CAN, AND HE'S THE ONE WITH THE MAP! THERE'S NO OTHER CHOICE!
JACK MAY NOT BE ONE OF US YET, BUT I WON'T LET HIM BE TORN TO BLOODY SHREDS WHILE YOU BOW AND SCRAPE BEFORE HIS TORMENTOR!
LISTEN TO ME, YOU MORON!
HASTINGS IS JUST SHIT IN A SILK STOCKING! I'D GIVE MY LAST LEG TO SLICE HIS GUT OPEN! BUT IF I HAVE TO SLIT THE THROAT OF ONE OF US SO THAT NOBLEMAN TAKES US FOR HONEST SAILORS FOR A FEW MORE DAYS, I WON'T HESITATE FOR A SECOND!!
SO, YES, JACK WILL BE TAUGHT A LESSON AND LEARN THE COST OF DISOBEYING. HE'LL CONFESS AFTER THE SECOND LASH AND HE'LL GET OFF WITH THREE DAYS' BED REST...
AS FOR US, MY FRIENDS, WE WILL DO WHAT'S TOUGHEST FOR MEN LIKE US. NOT ACT. NO; THAT WE DO WITH EASE.
NO... WE WILL ENDURE.
THAT'S THE PRICE WE HAVE TO PAY FOR THIS JOURNEY.
18-

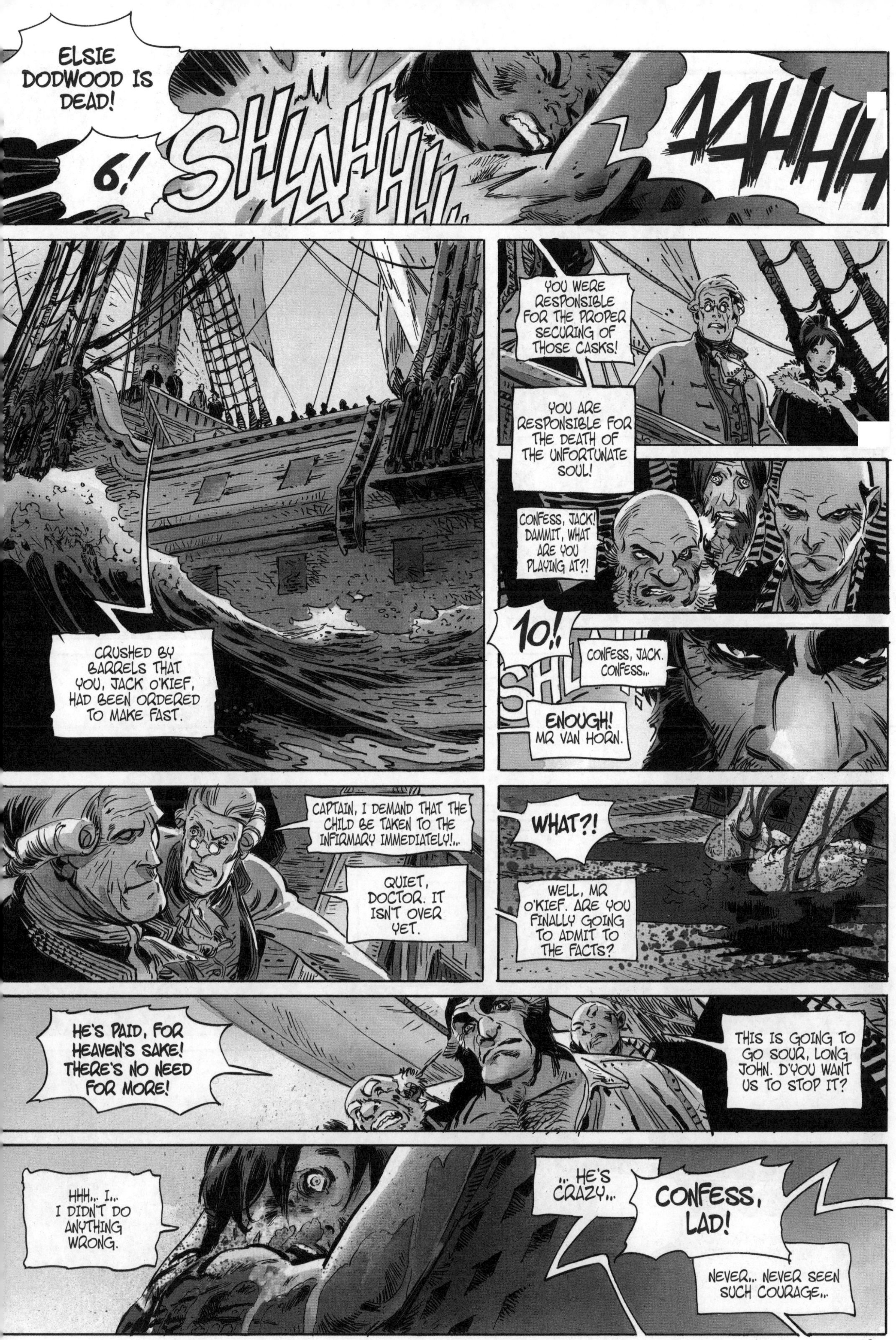
ELSIE DODWOOD IS DEAD!
6!
SHLAHHH
AAHHH
YOU WERE RESPONSIBLE FOR THE PROPER SECURING OF THOSE CASKS!
YOU ARE RESPONSIBLE FOR THE DEATH OF THE UNFORTUNATE SOUL!
CRUSHED BY BARRELS THAT YOU, JACK O'KIEF, HAD BEEN ORDERED TO MAKE FAST.
CONFESS, JACK! DAMMIT, WHAT ARE YOU PLAYING AT?!
10!
SHL
CONFESS, JACK. CONFESS...
ENOUGH! MR VAN HORN.
CAPTAIN, I DEMAND THAT THE CHILD BE TAKEN TO THE INFIRMARY IMMEDIATELY!...
QUIET, DOCTOR. IT ISN'T OVER YET.
WHAT?!
WELL, MR O'KIEF. ARE YOU FINALLY GOING TO ADMIT TO THE FACTS?
HE'S PAID, FOR HEAVEN'S SAKE! THERE'S NO NEED FOR MORE!
THIS IS GOING TO GO SOUR, LONG JOHN. D'YOU WANT US TO STOP IT?
HHH... I... I DIDN'T DO ANYTHING WRONG.
... HE'S CRAZY...
CONFESS, LAD!
NEVER... NEVER SEEN SUCH COURAGE...

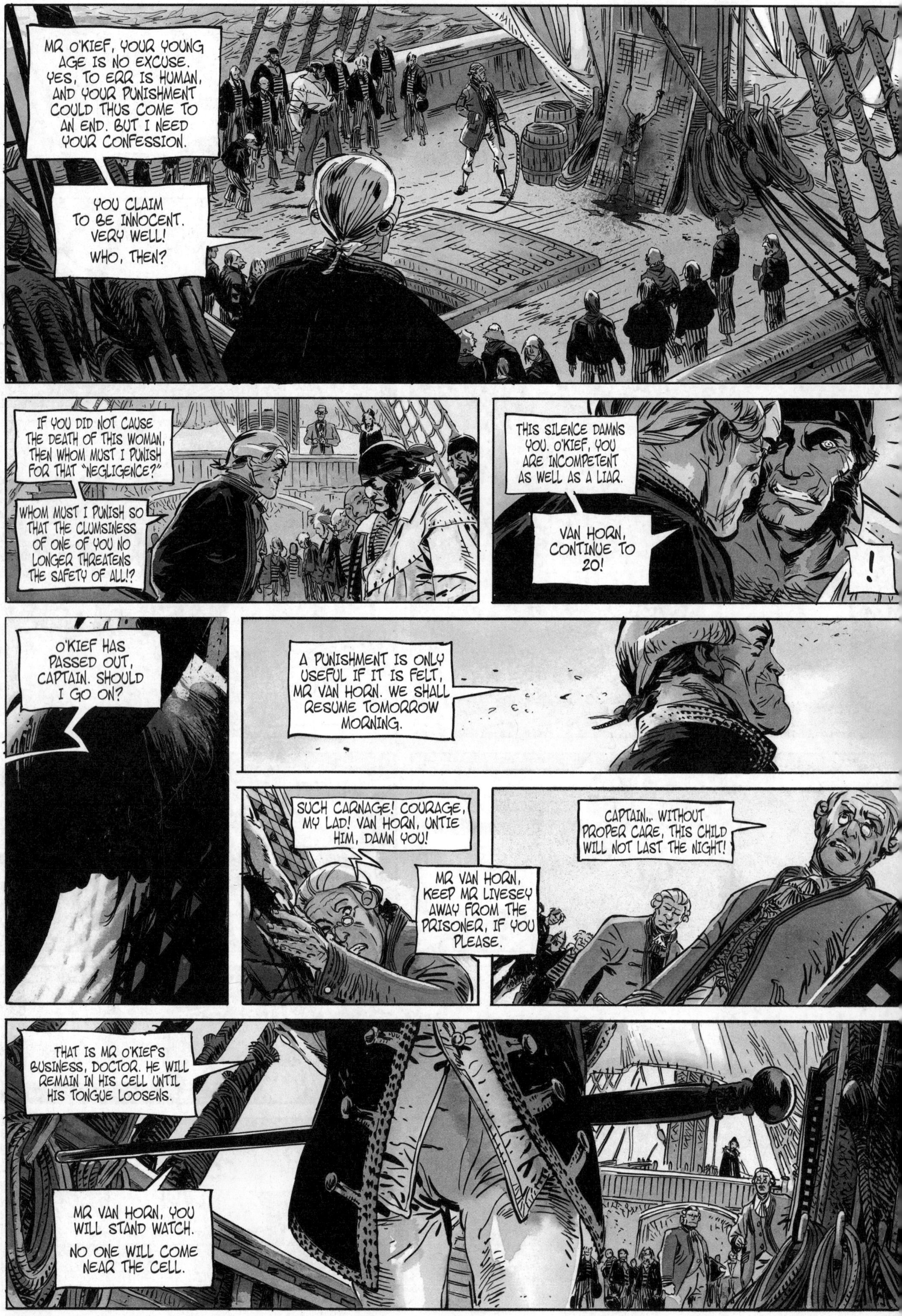
MR O'KIEF, YOUR YOUNG AGE IS NO EXCUSE. YES, TO ERR IS HUMAN, AND YOUR PUNISHMENT COULD THUS COME TO AN END. BUT I NEED YOUR CONFESSION.
YOU CLAIM TO BE INNOCENT. VERY WELL!
WHO, THEN?
IF YOU DID NOT CAUSE THE DEATH OF THIS WOMAN, THEN WHOM MUST I PUNISH FOR THAT "NEGLIGENCE?"
WHOM MUST I PUNISH SO THAT THE CLUMSINESS OF ONE OF YOU NO LONGER THREATENS THE SAFETY OF ALL!?
THIS SILENCE DAMNS YOU. O'KIEF, YOU ARE INCOMPETENT AS WELL AS A LIAR.
VAN HORN, CONTINUE TO 20!
!
O'KIEF HAS PASSED OUT, CAPTAIN. SHOULD I GO ON?
A PUNISHMENT IS ONLY USEFUL IF IT IS FELT, MR VAN HORN. WE SHALL RESUME TOMORROW MORNING.
SUCH CARNAGE! COURAGE, MY LAD! VAN HORN, UNTIE HIM, DAMN YOU!
MR VAN HORN, KEEP MR LIVESEY AWAY FROM THE PRISONER, IF YOU PLEASE.
CAPTAIN... WITHOUT PROPER CARE, THIS CHILD WILL NOT LAST THE NIGHT!
THAT IS MR O'KIEF'S BUSINESS, DOCTOR. HE WILL REMAIN IN HIS CELL UNTIL HIS TONGUE LOOSENS.
MR VAN HORN, YOU WILL STAND WATCH.
NO ONE WILL COME NEAR THE CELL.

20

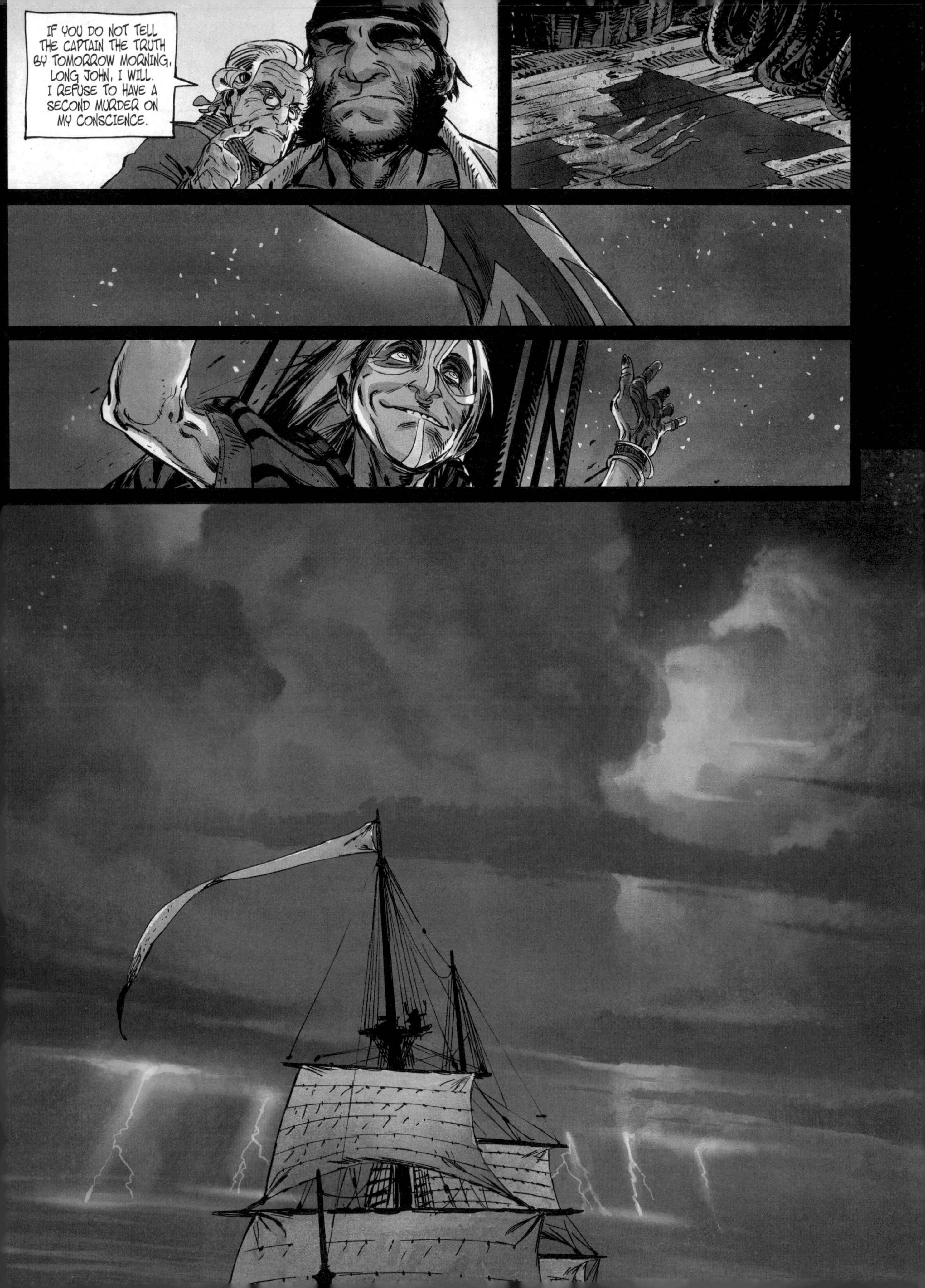
IF YOU DO NOT TELL THE CAPTAIN THE TRUTH BY TOMORROW MORNING, LONG JOHN, I WILL. I REFUSE TO HAVE A SECOND MURDER ON MY CONSCIENCE.

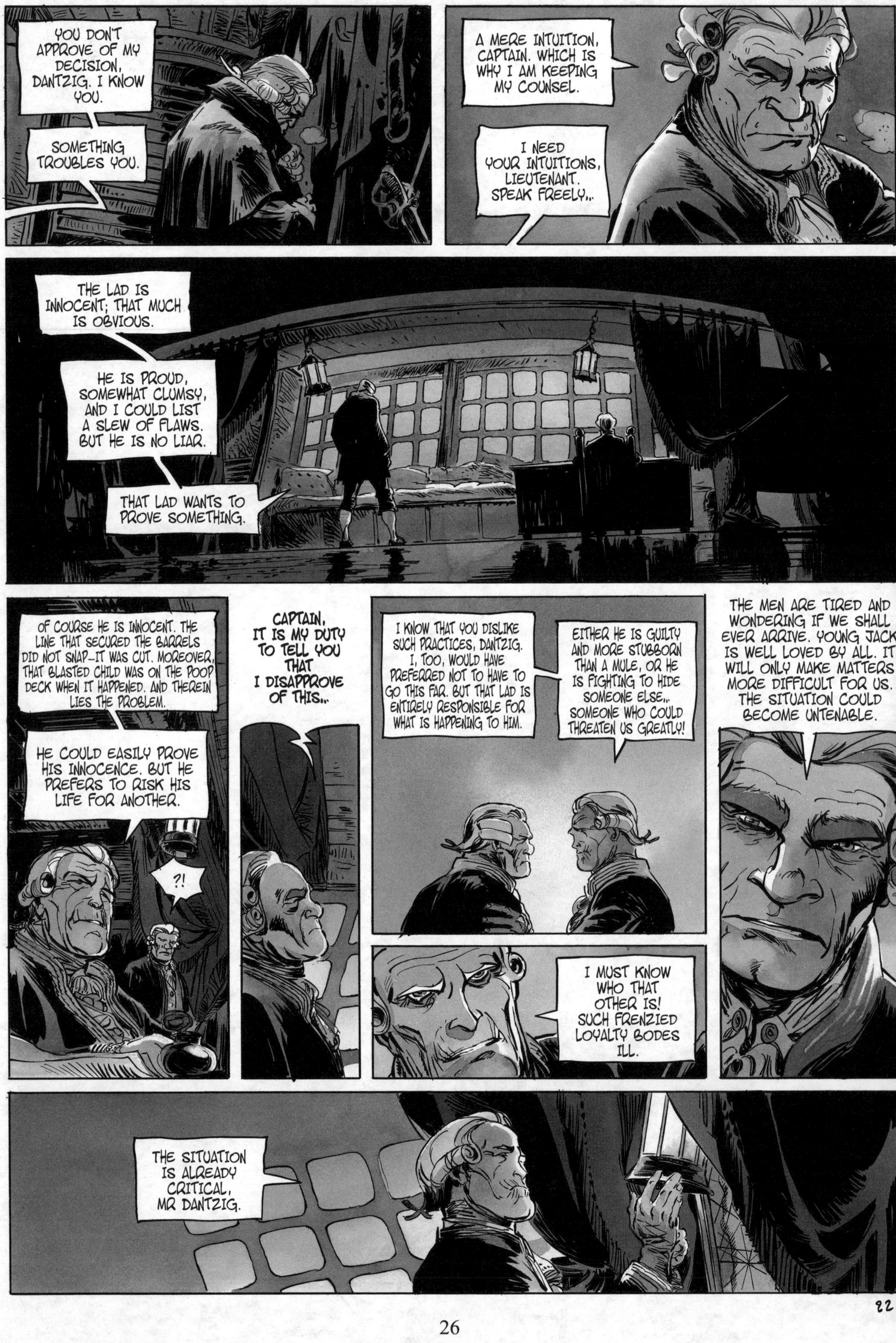
YOU DON'T APPROVE OF MY DECISION, DANTZIG. I KNOW YOU.
SOMETHING TROUBLES YOU.
A MERE INTUITION, CAPTAIN. WHICH IS WHY I AM KEEPING MY COUNSEL.
I NEED YOUR INTUITIONS, LIEUTENANT. SPEAK FREELY...
THE LAD IS INNOCENT; THAT MUCH IS OBVIOUS.
HE IS PROUD, SOMEWHAT CLUMSY, AND I COULD LIST A SLEW OF FLAWS. BUT HE IS NO LIAR.
THAT LAD WANTS TO PROVE SOMETHING.
OF COURSE HE IS INNOCENT. THE LINE THAT SECURED THE BARRELS DID NOT SNAP–IT WAS CUT. MOREOVER, THAT BLASTED CHILD WAS ON THE POOP DECK WHEN IT HAPPENED. AND THEREIN LIES THE PROBLEM.
HE COULD EASILY PROVE HIS INNOCENCE. BUT HE PREFERS TO RISK HIS LIFE FOR ANOTHER.
?!
CAPTAIN, IT IS MY DUTY TO TELL YOU THAT I DISAPPROVE OF THIS...
I KNOW THAT YOU DISLIKE SUCH PRACTICES, DANTZIG. I, TOO, WOULD HAVE PREFERRED NOT TO HAVE TO GO THIS FAR. BUT THAT LAD IS ENTIRELY RESPONSIBLE FOR WHAT IS HAPPENING TO HIM.
EITHER HE IS GUILTY AND MORE STUBBORN THAN A MULE, OR HE IS FIGHTING TO HIDE SOMEONE ELSE... SOMEONE WHO COULD THREATEN US GREATLY!
I MUST KNOW WHO THAT OTHER IS! SUCH FRENZIED LOYALTY BODES ILL.
THE MEN ARE TIRED AND WONDERING IF WE SHALL EVER ARRIVE. YOUNG JACK IS WELL LOVED BY ALL. IT WILL ONLY MAKE MATTERS MORE DIFFICULT FOR US. THE SITUATION COULD BECOME UNTENABLE.
THE SITUATION IS ALREADY CRITICAL, MR DANTZIG.
22

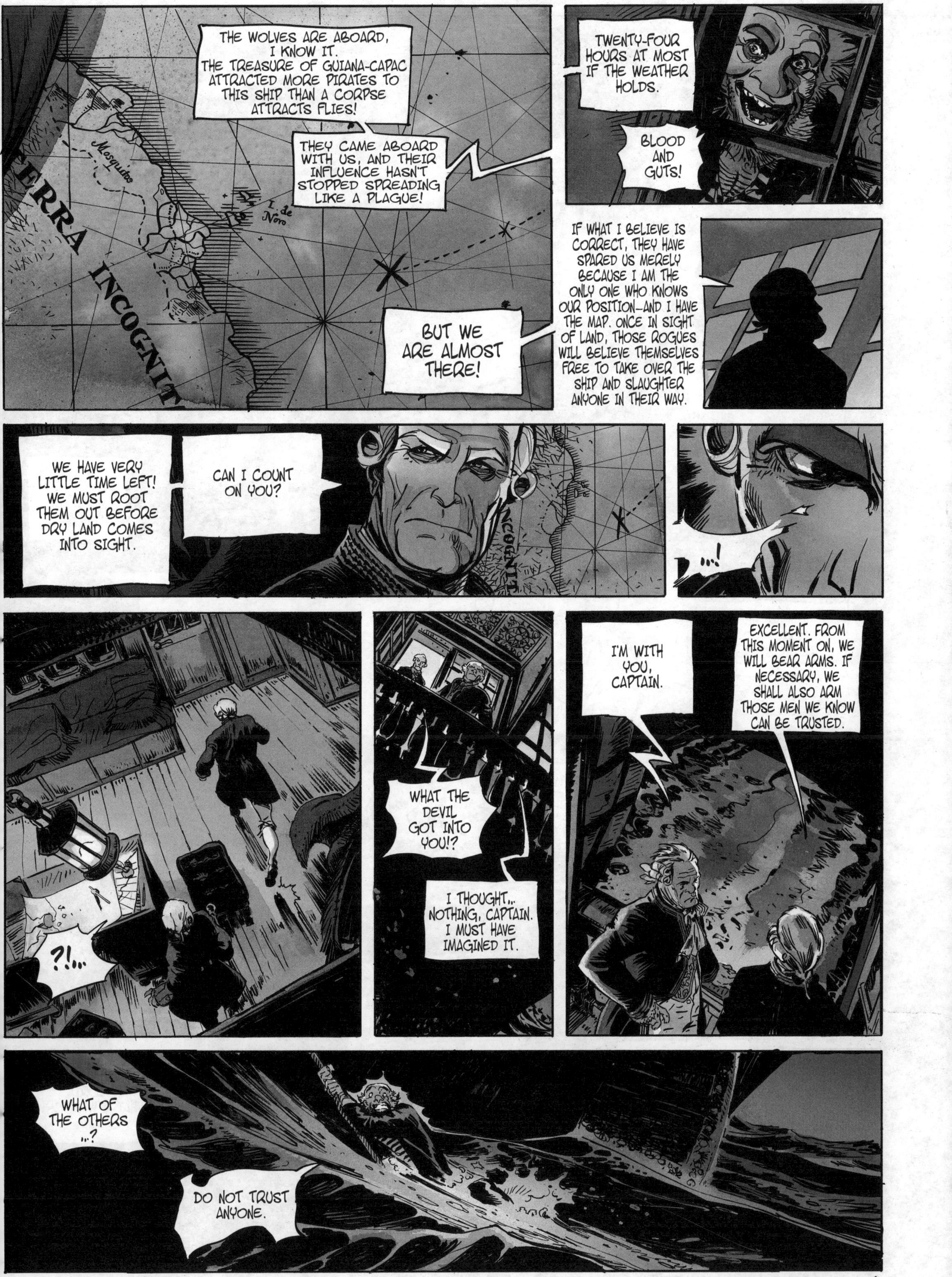
THE WOLVES ARE ABOARD, I KNOW IT. THE TREASURE OF GUIANA-CAPAC ATTRACTED MORE PIRATES TO THIS SHIP THAN A CORPSE ATTRACTS FLIES!
THEY CAME ABOARD WITH US, AND THEIR INFLUENCE HASN'T STOPPED SPREADING LIKE A PLAGUE!
TERRA INCOGNITA
Mosquitos
I. de Noro
BUT WE ARE ALMOST THERE!
TWENTY-FOUR HOURS AT MOST IF THE WEATHER HOLDS.
BLOOD AND GUTS!
IF WHAT I BELIEVE IS CORRECT, THEY HAVE SPARED US MERELY BECAUSE I AM THE ONLY ONE WHO KNOWS OUR POSITION–AND I HAVE THE MAP. ONCE IN SIGHT OF LAND, THOSE ROGUES WILL BELIEVE THEMSELVES FREE TO TAKE OVER THE SHIP AND SLAUGHTER ANYONE IN THEIR WAY.
WE HAVE VERY LITTLE TIME LEFT! WE MUST ROOT THEM OUT BEFORE DRY LAND COMES INTO SIGHT.
CAN I COUNT ON YOU?
...!
?!...
WHAT THE DEVIL GOT INTO YOU!?
I THOUGHT... NOTHING, CAPTAIN. I MUST HAVE IMAGINED IT.
I'M WITH YOU, CAPTAIN.
EXCELLENT. FROM THIS MOMENT ON, WE WILL BEAR ARMS. IF NECESSARY, WE SHALL ALSO ARM THOSE MEN WE KNOW CAN BE TRUSTED.
WHAT OF THE OTHERS ...?
DO NOT TRUST ANYONE.

23-

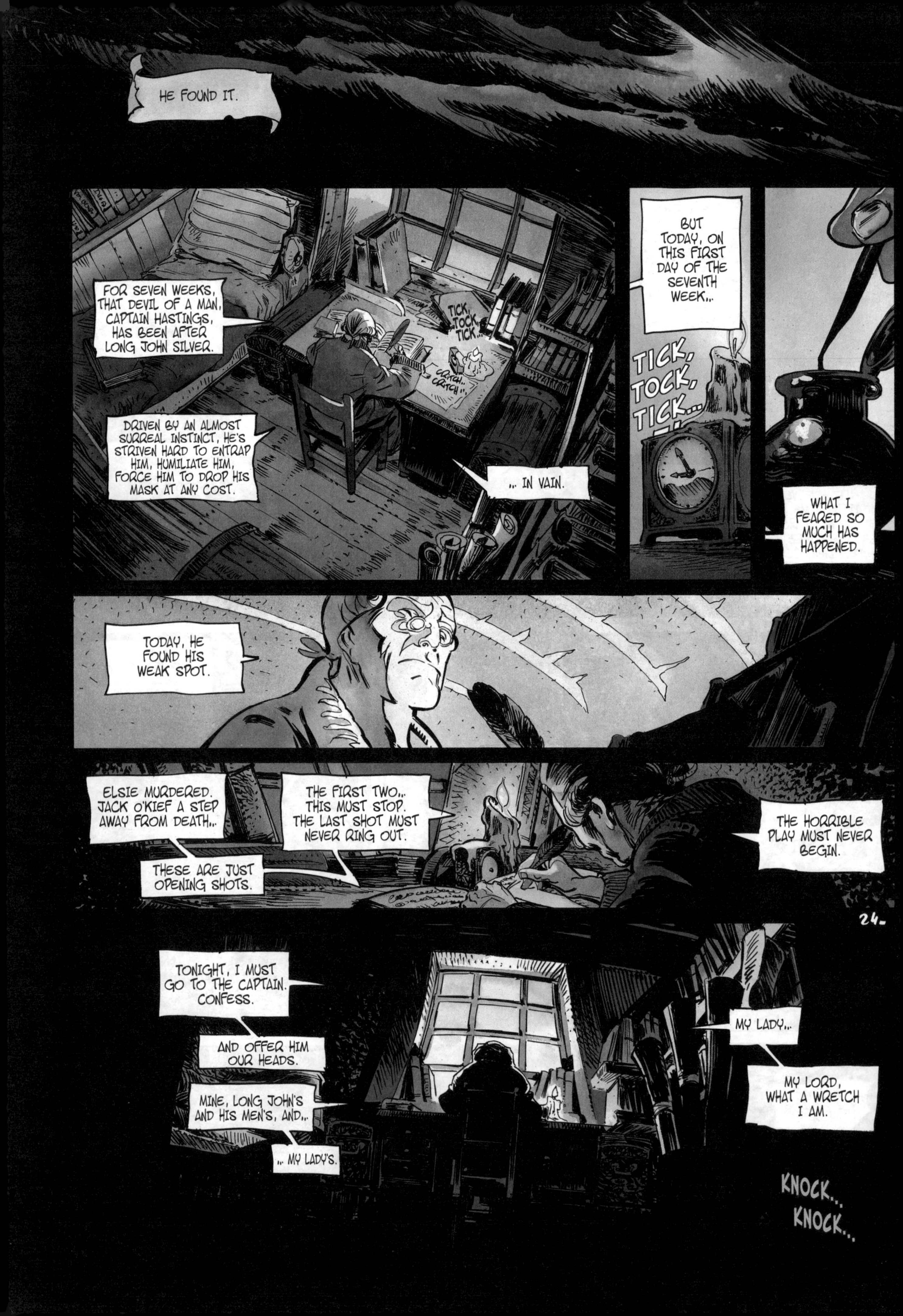
HE FOUND IT.
FOR SEVEN WEEKS, THAT DEVIL OF A MAN, CAPTAIN HASTINGS, HAS BEEN AFTER LONG JOHN SILVER.
TICK TOCK TICK...
CRATCH.. CRATCH
DRIVEN BY AN ALMOST SURREAL INSTINCT, HE'S STRIVEN HARD TO ENTRAP HIM, HUMILIATE HIM, FORCE HIM TO DROP HIS MASK AT ANY COST.
... IN VAIN.
BUT TODAY, ON THIS FIRST DAY OF THE SEVENTH WEEK...
TICK, TOCK, TICK...
WHAT I FEARED SO MUCH HAS HAPPENED.
TODAY, HE FOUND HIS WEAK SPOT.
ELSIE MURDERED. JACK O'KIEF A STEP AWAY FROM DEATH...
THESE ARE JUST OPENING SHOTS.
THE FIRST TWO... THIS MUST STOP. THE LAST SHOT MUST NEVER RING OUT.
THE HORRIBLE PLAY MUST NEVER BEGIN.
TONIGHT, I MUST GO TO THE CAPTAIN. CONFESS.
AND OFFER HIM OUR HEADS.
MINE, LONG JOHN'S AND HIS MEN'S, AND...
... MY LADY'S.
MY LADY...
MY LORD, WHAT A WRETCH I AM.
KNOCK...
KNOCK...

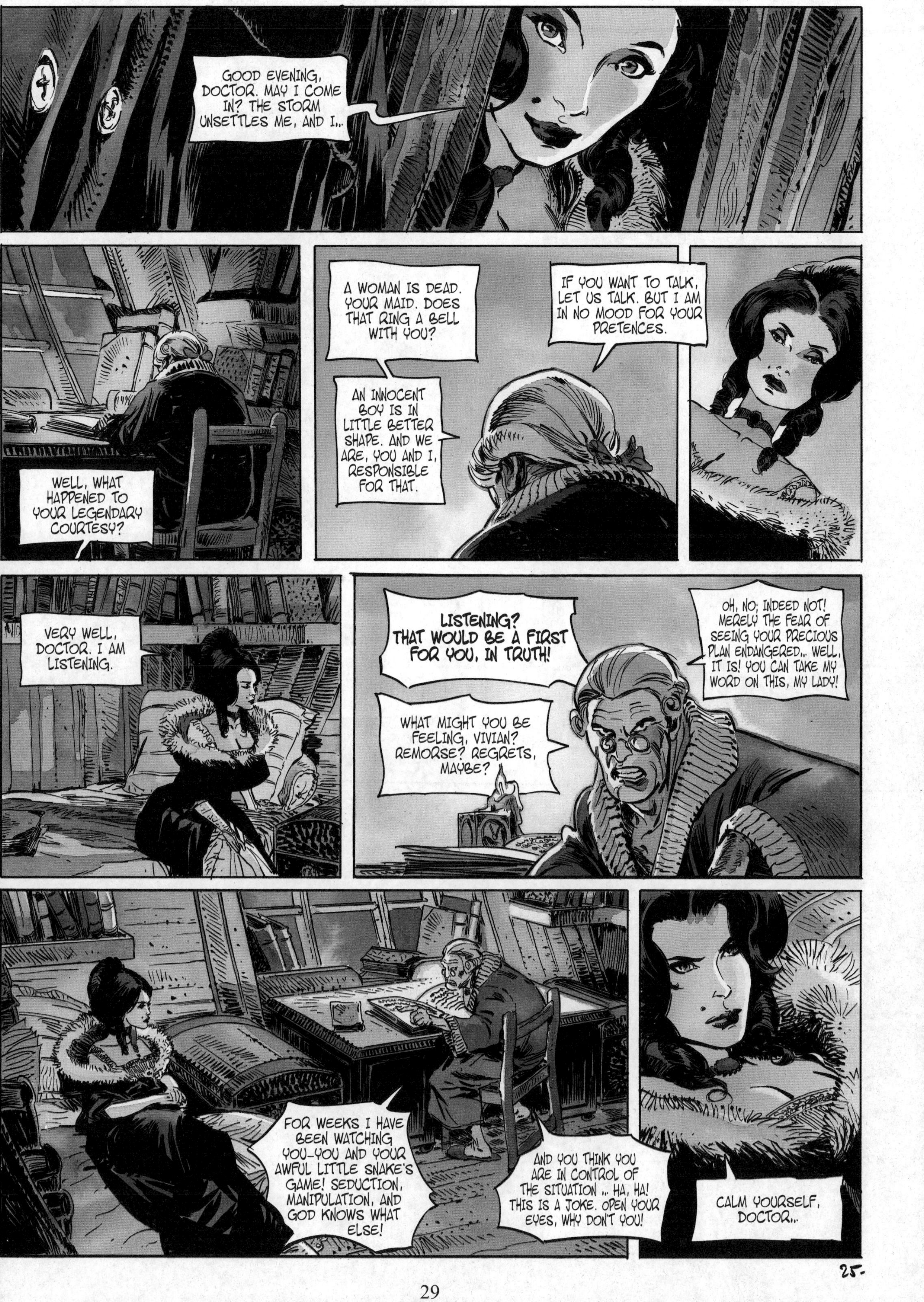
GOOD EVENING, DOCTOR. MAY I COME IN? THE STORM UNSETTLES ME, AND I...
WELL, WHAT HAPPENED TO YOUR LEGENDARY COURTESY?
A WOMAN IS DEAD. YOUR MAID. DOES THAT RING A BELL WITH YOU?
AN INNOCENT BOY IS IN LITTLE BETTER SHAPE. AND WE ARE, YOU AND I, RESPONSIBLE FOR THAT.
IF YOU WANT TO TALK, LET US TALK. BUT I AM IN NO MOOD FOR YOUR PRETENCES.
VERY WELL, DOCTOR. I AM LISTENING.
LISTENING? THAT WOULD BE A FIRST FOR YOU, IN TRUTH!
WHAT MIGHT YOU BE FEELING, VIVIAN? REMORSE? REGRETS, MAYBE?
OH, NO; INDEED NOT! MERELY THE FEAR OF SEEING YOUR PRECIOUS PLAN ENDANGERED... WELL, IT IS! YOU CAN TAKE MY WORD ON THIS, MY LADY!
FOR WEEKS I HAVE BEEN WATCHING YOU–YOU AND YOUR AWFUL LITTLE SNAKE'S GAME! SEDUCTION, MANIPULATION, AND GOD KNOWS WHAT ELSE!
AND YOU THINK YOU ARE IN CONTROL OF THE SITUATION .. HA, HA! THIS IS A JOKE. OPEN YOUR EYES, WHY DON'T YOU!
CALM YOURSELF, DOCTOR...
25-

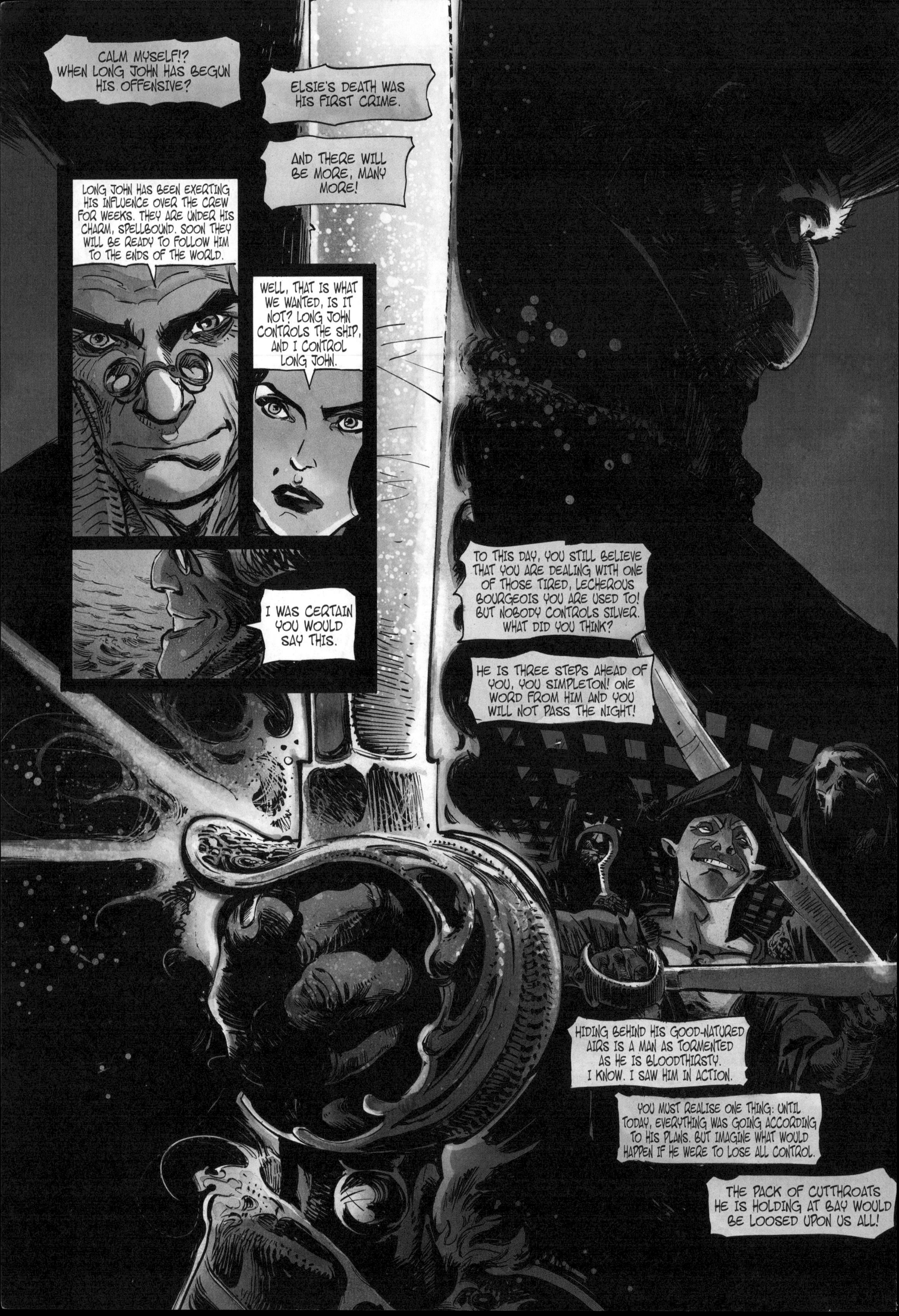

CALM MYSELF!? WHEN LONG JOHN HAS BEGUN HIS OFFENSIVE?
ELSIE'S DEATH WAS HIS FIRST CRIME.
AND THERE WILL BE MORE, MANY MORE!
LONG JOHN HAS BEEN EXERTING HIS INFLUENCE OVER THE CREW FOR WEEKS. THEY ARE UNDER HIS CHARM, SPELLBOUND. SOON THEY WILL BE READY TO FOLLOW HIM TO THE ENDS OF THE WORLD.
WELL, THAT IS WHAT WE WANTED, IS IT NOT? LONG JOHN CONTROLS THE SHIP, AND I CONTROL LONG JOHN.
I WAS CERTAIN YOU WOULD SAY THIS.
TO THIS DAY, YOU STILL BELIEVE THAT YOU ARE DEALING WITH ONE OF THOSE TIRED, LECHEROUS BOURGEOIS YOU ARE USED TO! BUT NOBODY CONTROLS SILVER. WHAT DID YOU THINK?
HE IS THREE STEPS AHEAD OF YOU, YOU SIMPLETON! ONE WORD FROM HIM AND YOU WILL NOT PASS THE NIGHT!
HIDING BEHIND HIS GOOD-NATURED AIRS IS A MAN AS TORMENTED AS HE IS BLOODTHIRSTY. I KNOW. I SAW HIM IN ACTION.
YOU MUST REALISE ONE THING: UNTIL TODAY, EVERYTHING WAS GOING ACCORDING TO HIS PLANS. BUT IMAGINE WHAT WOULD HAPPEN IF HE WERE TO LOSE ALL CONTROL.
THE PACK OF CUTTHROATS HE IS HOLDING AT BAY WOULD BE LOOSED UPON US ALL!

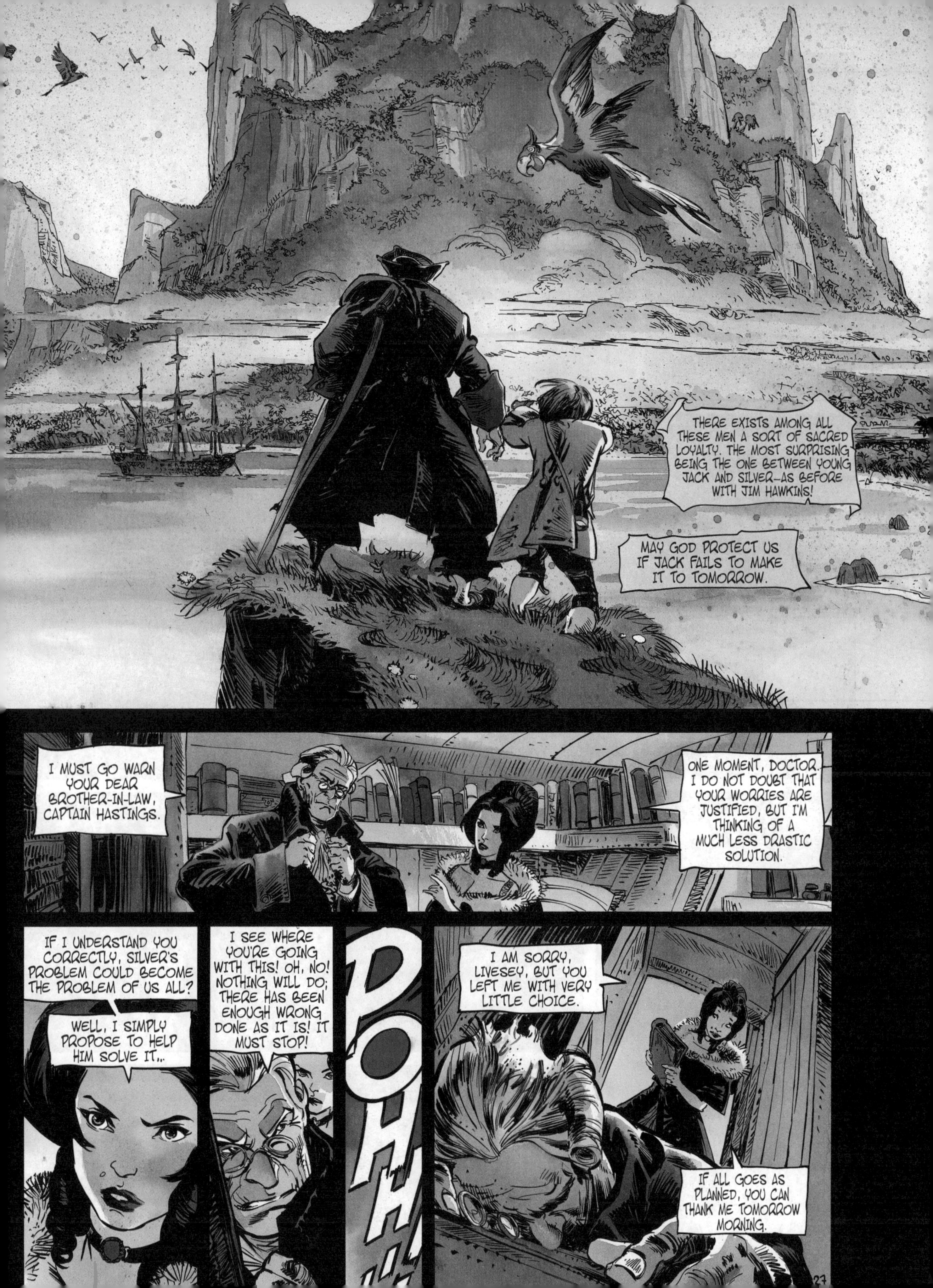

THERE EXISTS AMONG ALL THESE MEN A SORT OF SACRED LOYALTY. THE MOST SURPRISING BEING THE ONE BETWEEN YOUNG JACK AND SILVER–AS BEFORE WITH JIM HAWKINS!
MAY GOD PROTECT US IF JACK FAILS TO MAKE IT TO TOMORROW.
I MUST GO WARN YOUR DEAR BROTHER-IN-LAW, CAPTAIN HASTINGS.
ONE MOMENT, DOCTOR. I DO NOT DOUBT THAT YOUR WORRIES ARE JUSTIFIED, BUT I'M THINKING OF A MUCH LESS DRASTIC SOLUTION.
IF I UNDERSTAND YOU CORRECTLY, SILVER'S PROBLEM COULD BECOME THE PROBLEM OF US ALL?
WELL, I SIMPLY PROPOSE TO HELP HIM SOLVE IT...
I SEE WHERE YOU'RE GOING WITH THIS! OH, NO! NOTHING WILL DO; THERE HAS BEEN ENOUGH WRONG DONE AS IT IS! IT MUST STOP!
I AM SORRY, LIVESEY, BUT YOU LEFT ME WITH VERY LITTLE CHOICE.
IF ALL GOES AS PLANNED, YOU CAN THANK ME TOMORROW MORNING.

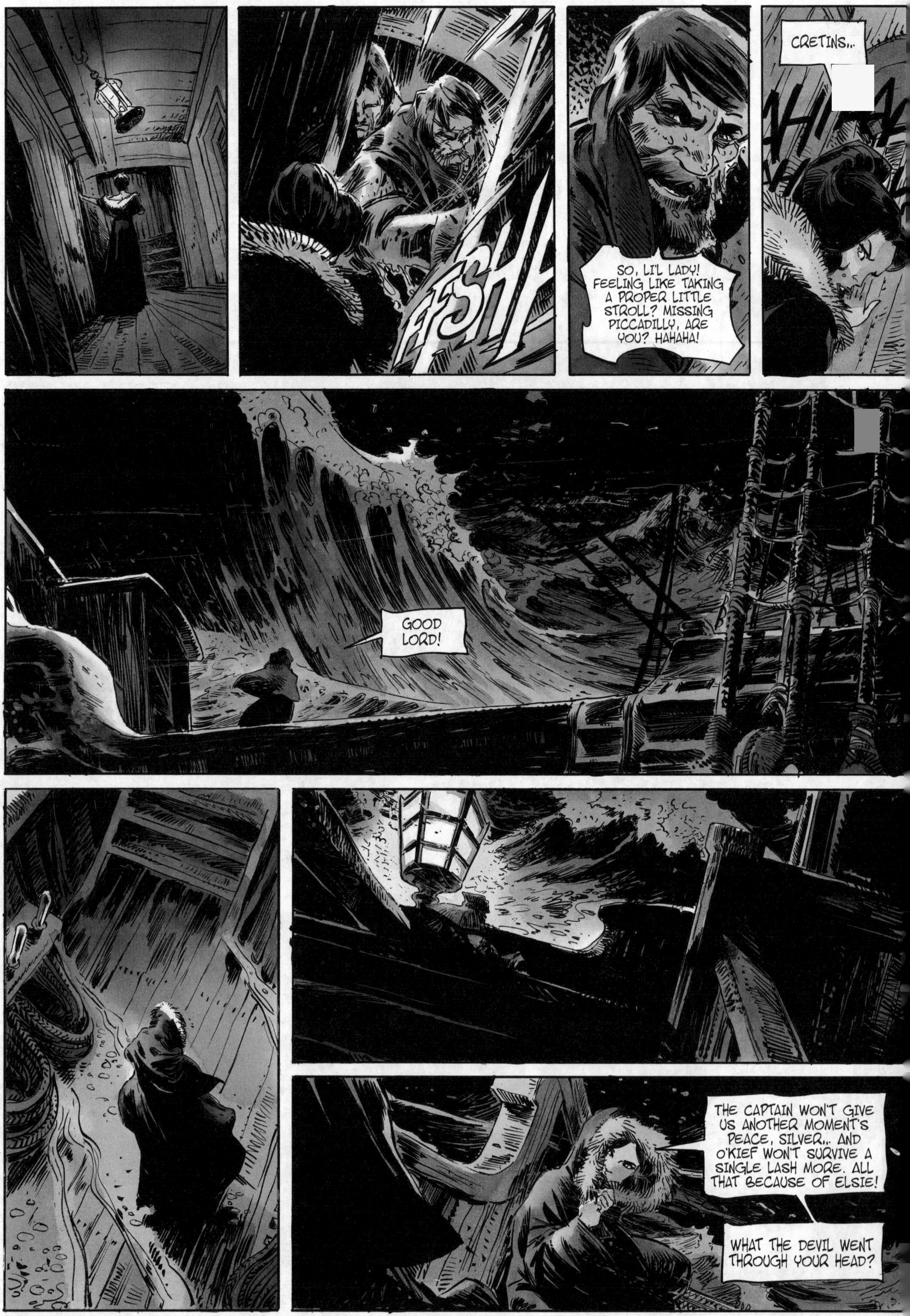

FFSHH
SO, LI'L LADY! FEELING LIKE TAKING A PROPER LITTLE STROLL? MISSING PICCADILLY, ARE YOU? HAHAHA!
CRETINS...
GOOD LORD!
THE CAPTAIN WON'T GIVE US ANOTHER MOMENT'S PEACE, SILVER... AND O'KIEF WON'T SURVIVE A SINGLE LASH MORE. ALL THAT BECAUSE OF ELSIE!
WHAT THE DEVIL WENT THROUGH YOUR HEAD?

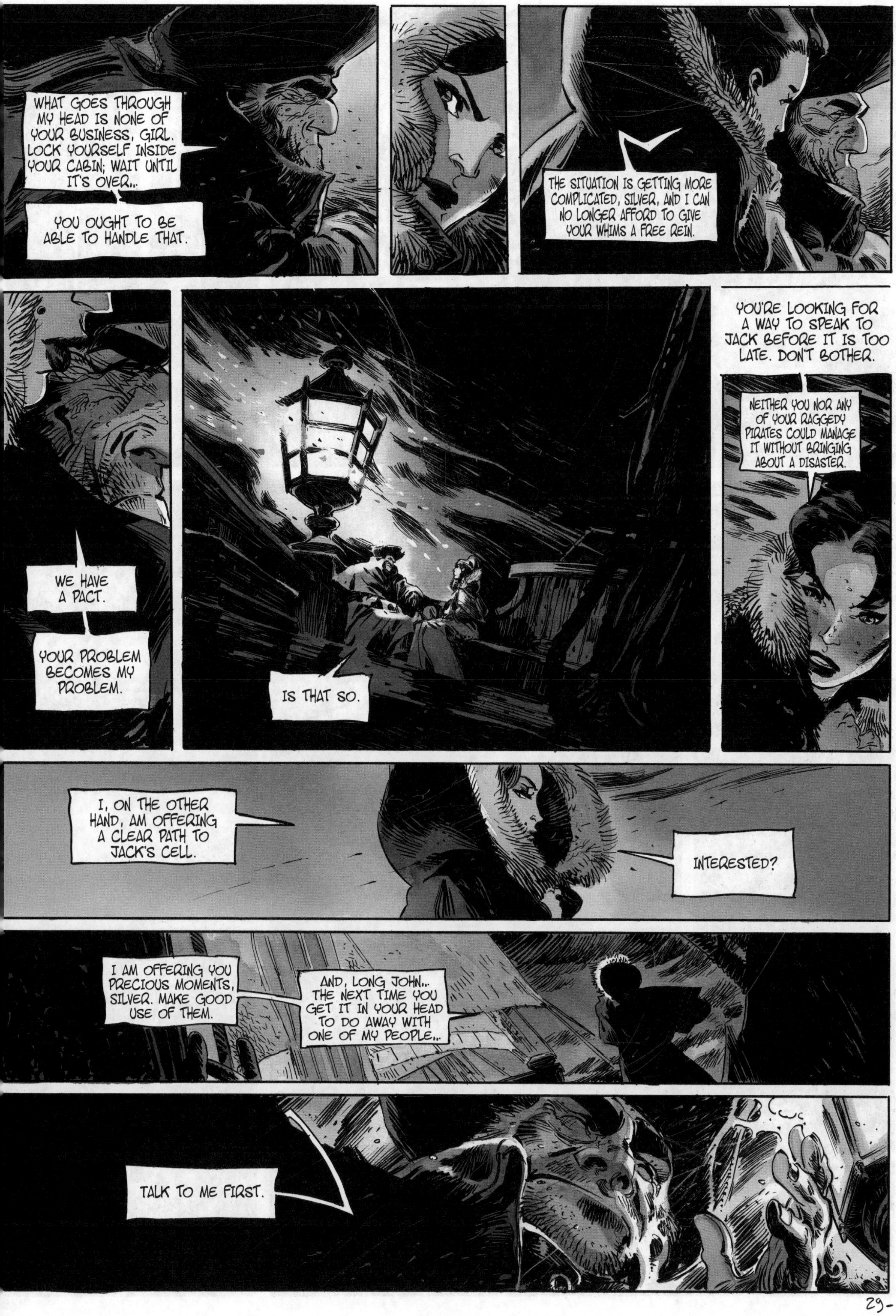
WHAT GOES THROUGH MY HEAD IS NONE OF YOUR BUSINESS, GIRL. LOCK YOURSELF INSIDE YOUR CABIN; WAIT UNTIL IT'S OVER...
YOU OUGHT TO BE ABLE TO HANDLE THAT.
THE SITUATION IS GETTING MORE COMPLICATED, SILVER, AND I CAN NO LONGER AFFORD TO GIVE YOUR WHIMS A FREE REIN.
YOU'RE LOOKING FOR A WAY TO SPEAK TO JACK BEFORE IT IS TOO LATE. DON'T BOTHER.
NEITHER YOU NOR ANY OF YOUR RAGGEDY PIRATES COULD MANAGE IT WITHOUT BRINGING ABOUT A DISASTER.
WE HAVE A PACT.
YOUR PROBLEM BECOMES MY PROBLEM.
IS THAT SO.
I, ON THE OTHER HAND, AM OFFERING A CLEAR PATH TO JACK'S CELL.
INTERESTED?
I AM OFFERING YOU PRECIOUS MOMENTS, SILVER. MAKE GOOD USE OF THEM.
AND, LONG JOHN... THE NEXT TIME YOU GET IT IN YOUR HEAD TO DO AWAY WITH ONE OF MY PEOPLE...
TALK TO ME FIRST.
29-

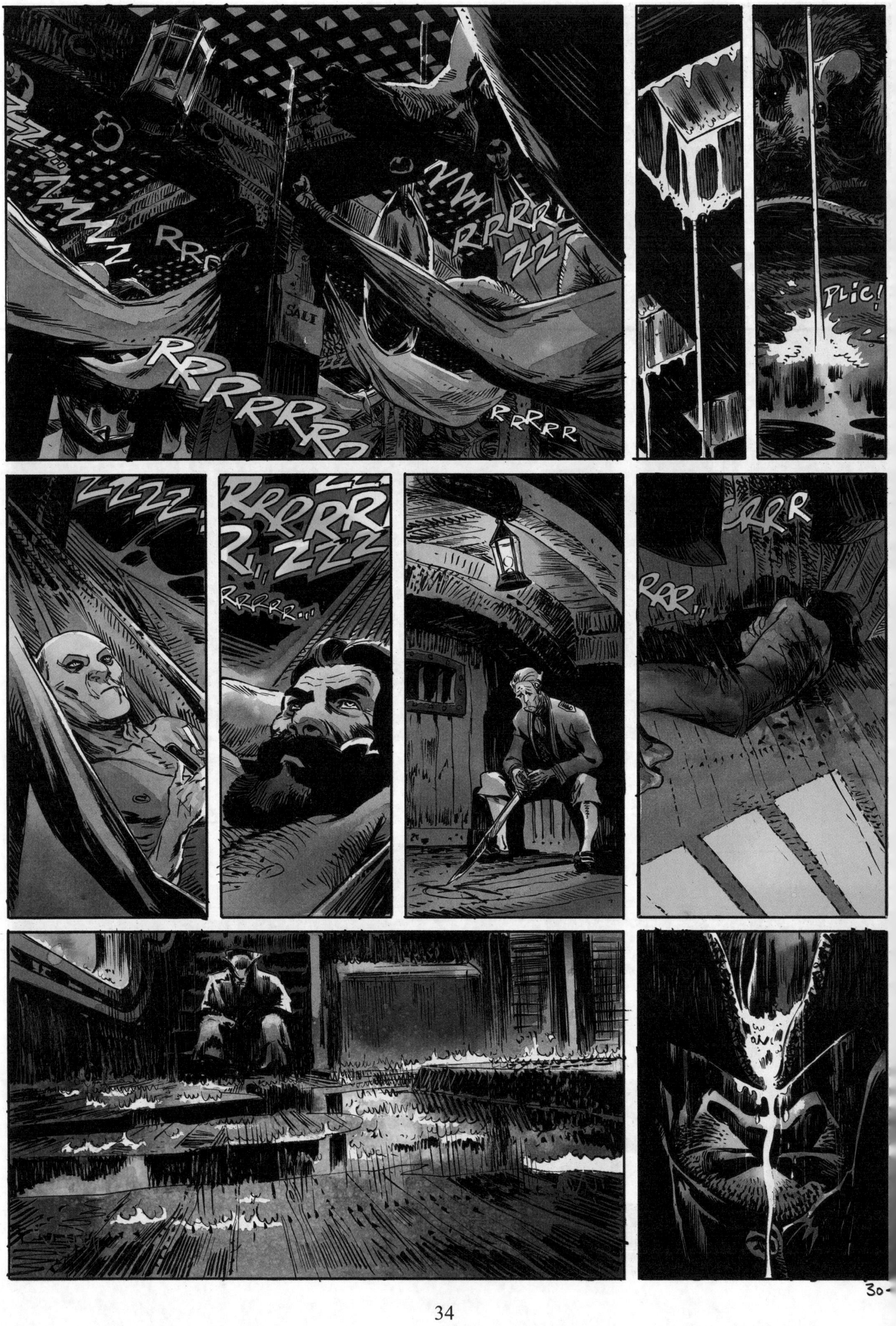
PLIC!
RRR
RRR,,

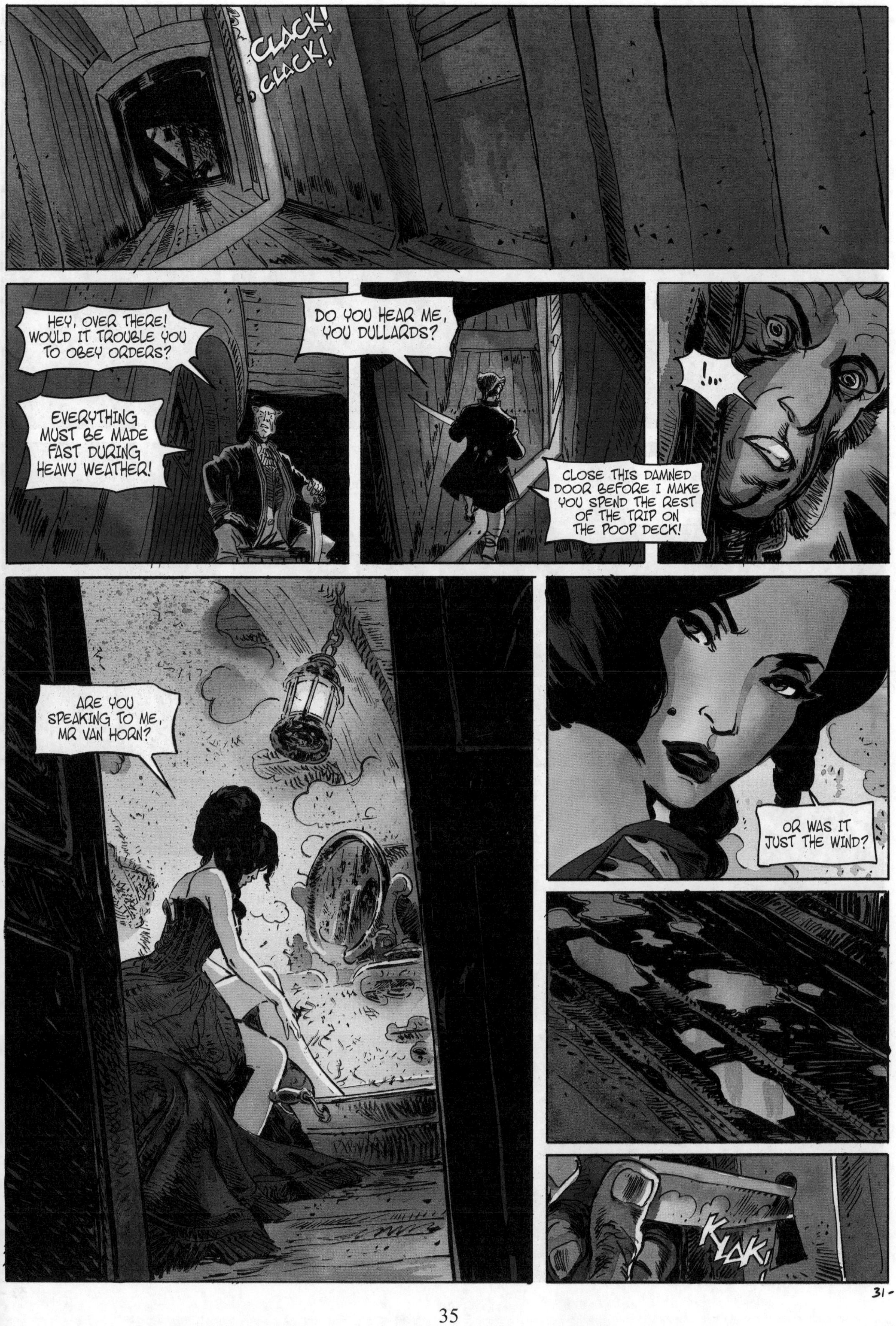
CLACK! CLACK!
HEY, OVER THERE! WOULD IT TROUBLE YOU TO OBEY ORDERS?
EVERYTHING MUST BE MADE FAST DURING HEAVY WEATHER!
DO YOU HEAR ME, YOU DULLARDS?
CLOSE THIS DAMNED DOOR BEFORE I MAKE YOU SPEND THE REST OF THE TRIP ON THE POOP DECK!
!...
ARE YOU SPEAKING TO ME, MR VAN HORN?
OR WAS IT JUST THE WIND?
KLAK!

31-

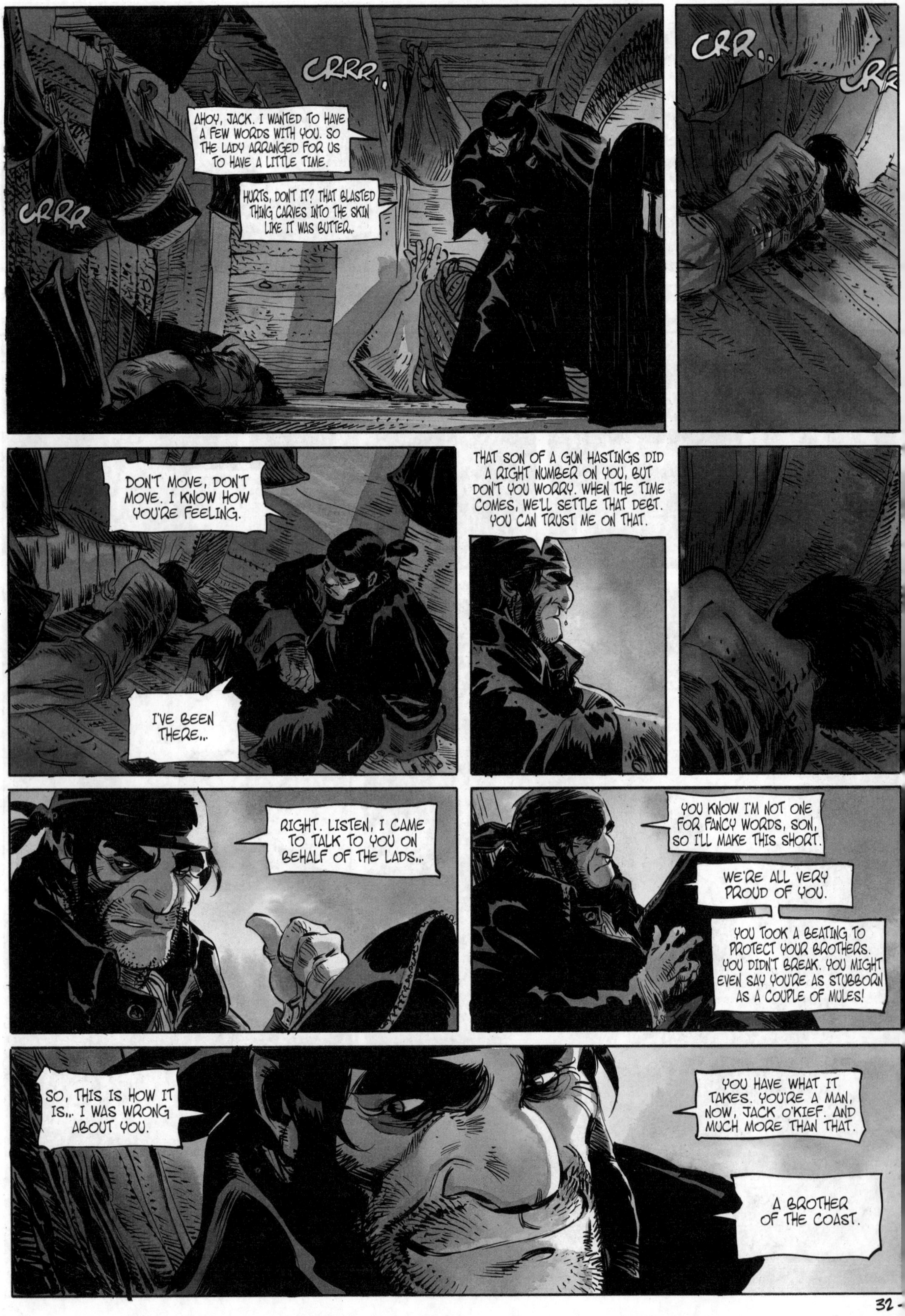
CRRR..
AHOY, JACK. I WANTED TO HAVE A FEW WORDS WITH YOU. SO THE LADY ARRANGED FOR US TO HAVE A LITTLE TIME.
HURTS, DON'T IT? THAT BLASTED THING CARVES INTO THE SKIN LIKE IT WAS BUTTER..
CRRR
CRR..
DON'T MOVE, DON'T MOVE. I KNOW HOW YOU'RE FEELING.
I'VE BEEN THERE...
THAT SON OF A GUN HASTINGS DID A RIGHT NUMBER ON YOU, BUT DON'T YOU WORRY. WHEN THE TIME COMES, WE'LL SETTLE THAT DEBT. YOU CAN TRUST ME ON THAT.
RIGHT. LISTEN, I CAME TO TALK TO YOU ON BEHALF OF THE LADS...
YOU KNOW I'M NOT ONE FOR FANCY WORDS, SON, SO I'LL MAKE THIS SHORT.
WE'RE ALL VERY PROUD OF YOU.
YOU TOOK A BEATING TO PROTECT YOUR BROTHERS. YOU DIDN'T BREAK. YOU MIGHT EVEN SAY YOU'RE AS STUBBORN AS A COUPLE OF MULES!
SO, THIS IS HOW IT IS... I WAS WRONG ABOUT YOU.
YOU HAVE WHAT IT TAKES. YOU'RE A MAN, NOW, JACK O'KIEF. AND MUCH MORE THAN THAT.
A BROTHER OF THE COAST.
32-

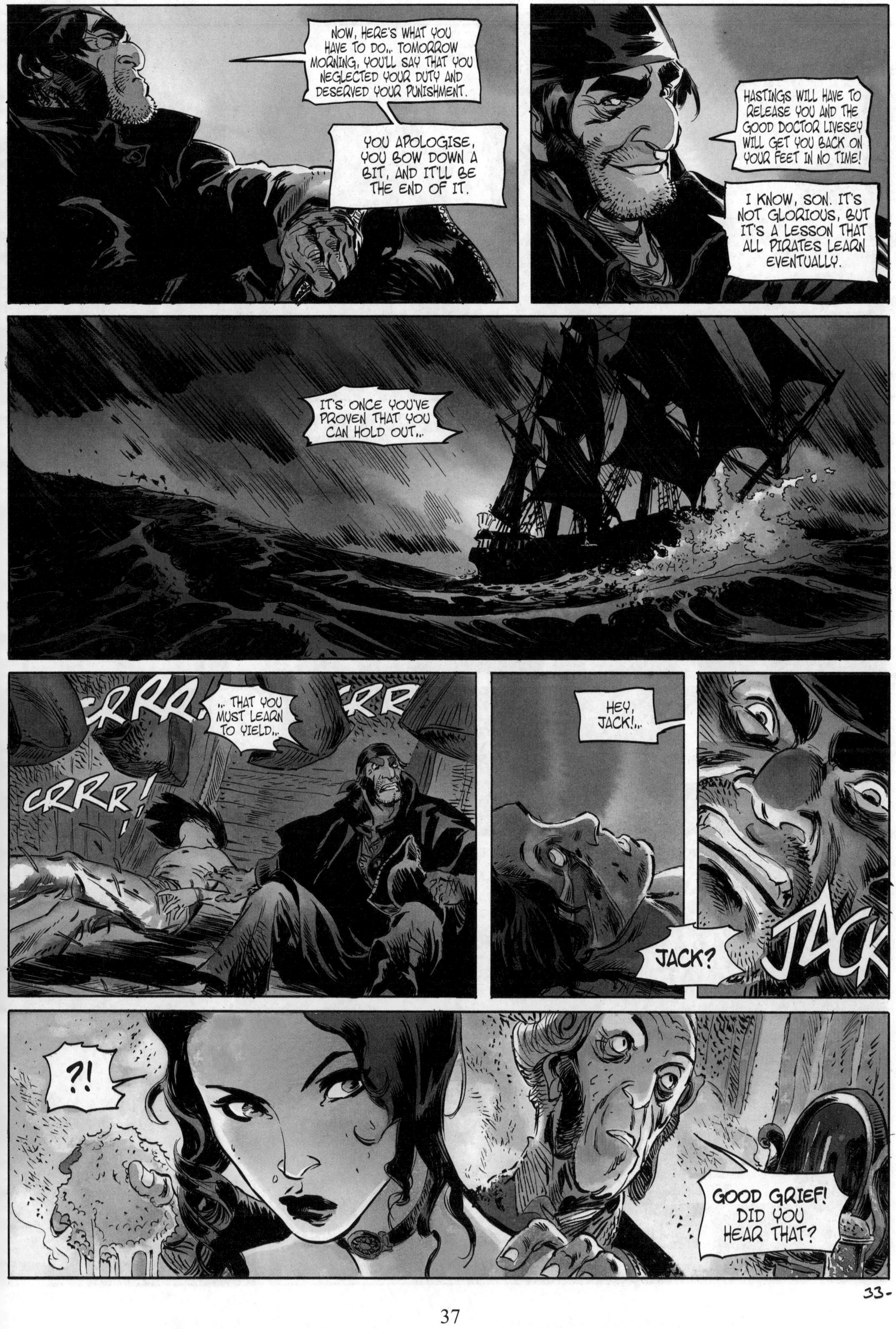
NOW, HERE'S WHAT YOU HAVE TO DO... TOMORROW MORNING, YOU'LL SAY THAT YOU NEGLECTED YOUR DUTY AND DESERVED YOUR PUNISHMENT.
YOU APOLOGISE, YOU BOW DOWN A BIT, AND IT'LL BE THE END OF IT.
HASTINGS WILL HAVE TO RELEASE YOU AND THE GOOD DOCTOR LIVESEY WILL GET YOU BACK ON YOUR FEET IN NO TIME!
I KNOW, SON. IT'S NOT GLORIOUS, BUT IT'S A LESSON THAT ALL PIRATES LEARN EVENTUALLY.
IT'S ONCE YOU'VE PROVEN THAT YOU CAN HOLD OUT...
CRRR!
... THAT YOU MUST LEARN TO YIELD...
CRRR!
HEY, JACK!...
JACK?
JACK
?!
GOOD GRIEF! DID YOU HEAR THAT?

33-

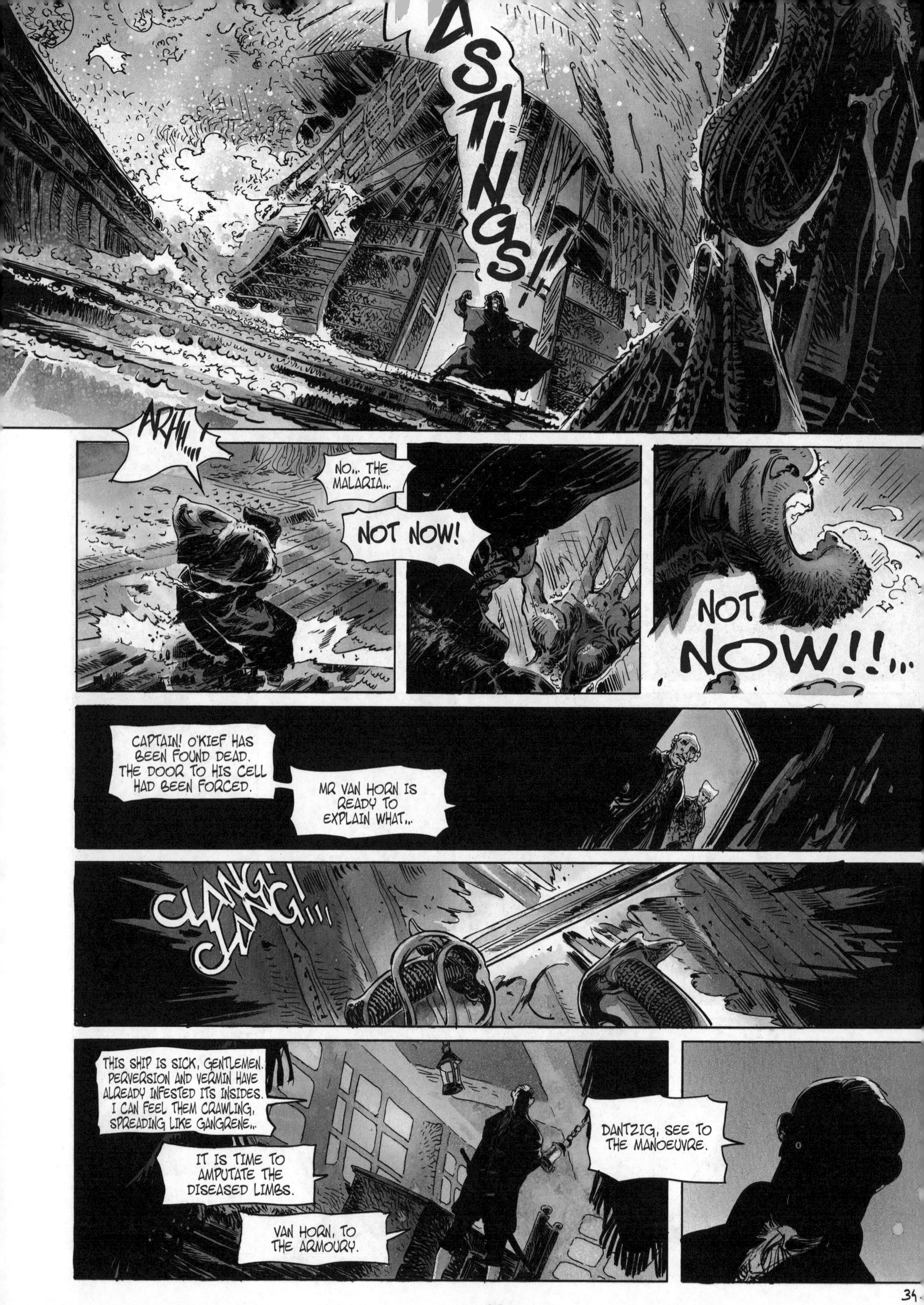
ASTINGS!!
ARHH...!
NO... THE MALARIA...
NOT NOW!
NOT NOW!!...
CAPTAIN! O'KIEF HAS BEEN FOUND DEAD. THE DOOR TO HIS CELL HAD BEEN FORCED.
MR VAN HORN IS READY TO EXPLAIN WHAT...
CLANG! CLANG!...
THIS SHIP IS SICK, GENTLEMEN. PERVERSION AND VERMIN HAVE ALREADY INFESTED ITS INSIDES. I CAN FEEL THEM CRAWLING, SPREADING LIKE GANGRENE...
IT IS TIME TO AMPUTATE THE DISEASED LIMBS.
VAN HORN, TO THE ARMOURY.
DANTZIG, SEE TO THE MANOEUVRE.
34

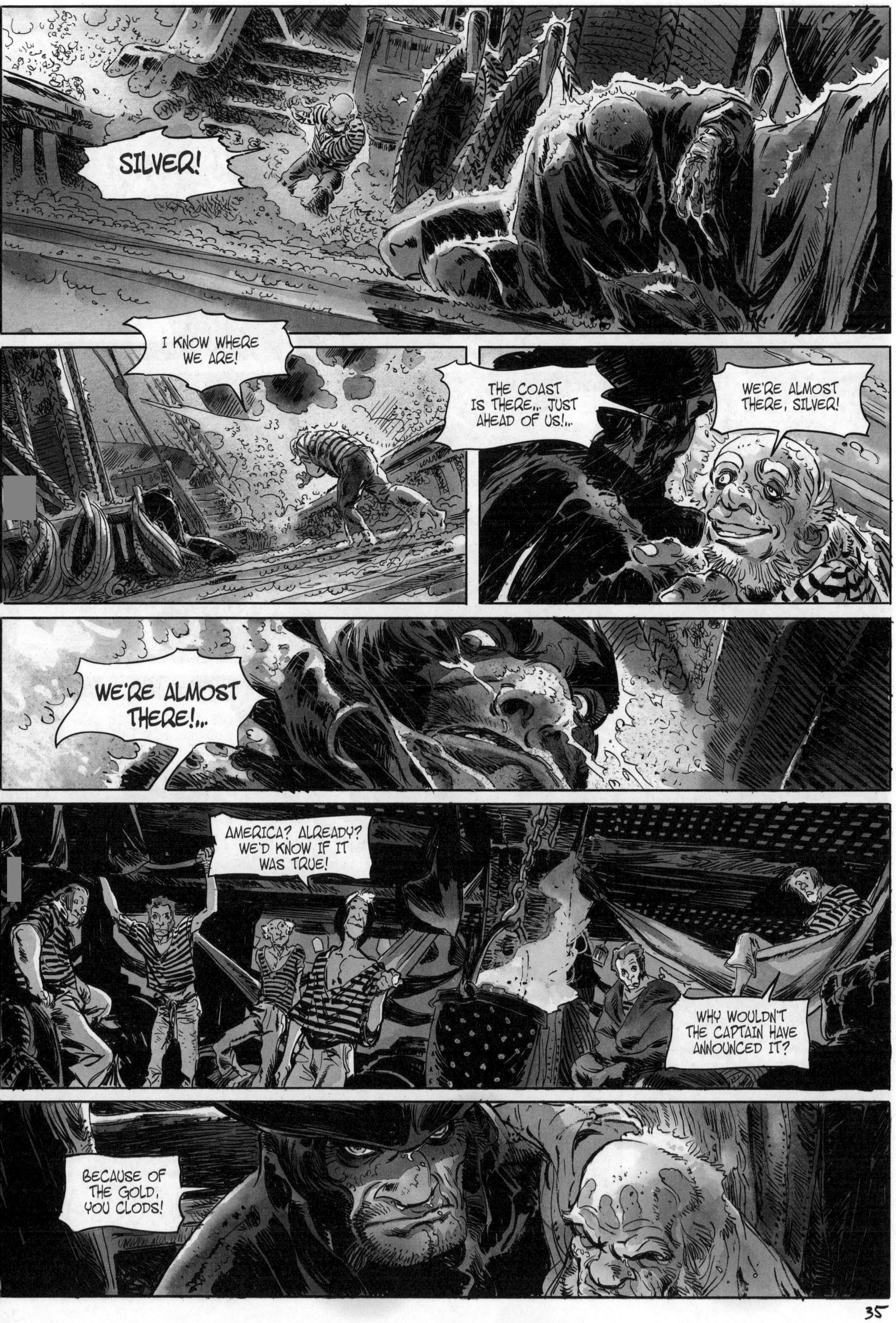
SILVER!
I KNOW WHERE WE ARE!
THE COAST IS THERE... JUST AHEAD OF US!...
WE'RE ALMOST THERE, SILVER!
WE'RE ALMOST THERE!...
AMERICA? ALREADY? WE'D KNOW IF IT WAS TRUE!
WHY WOULDN'T THE CAPTAIN HAVE ANNOUNCED IT?
BECAUSE OF THE GOLD, YOU CLODS!
35

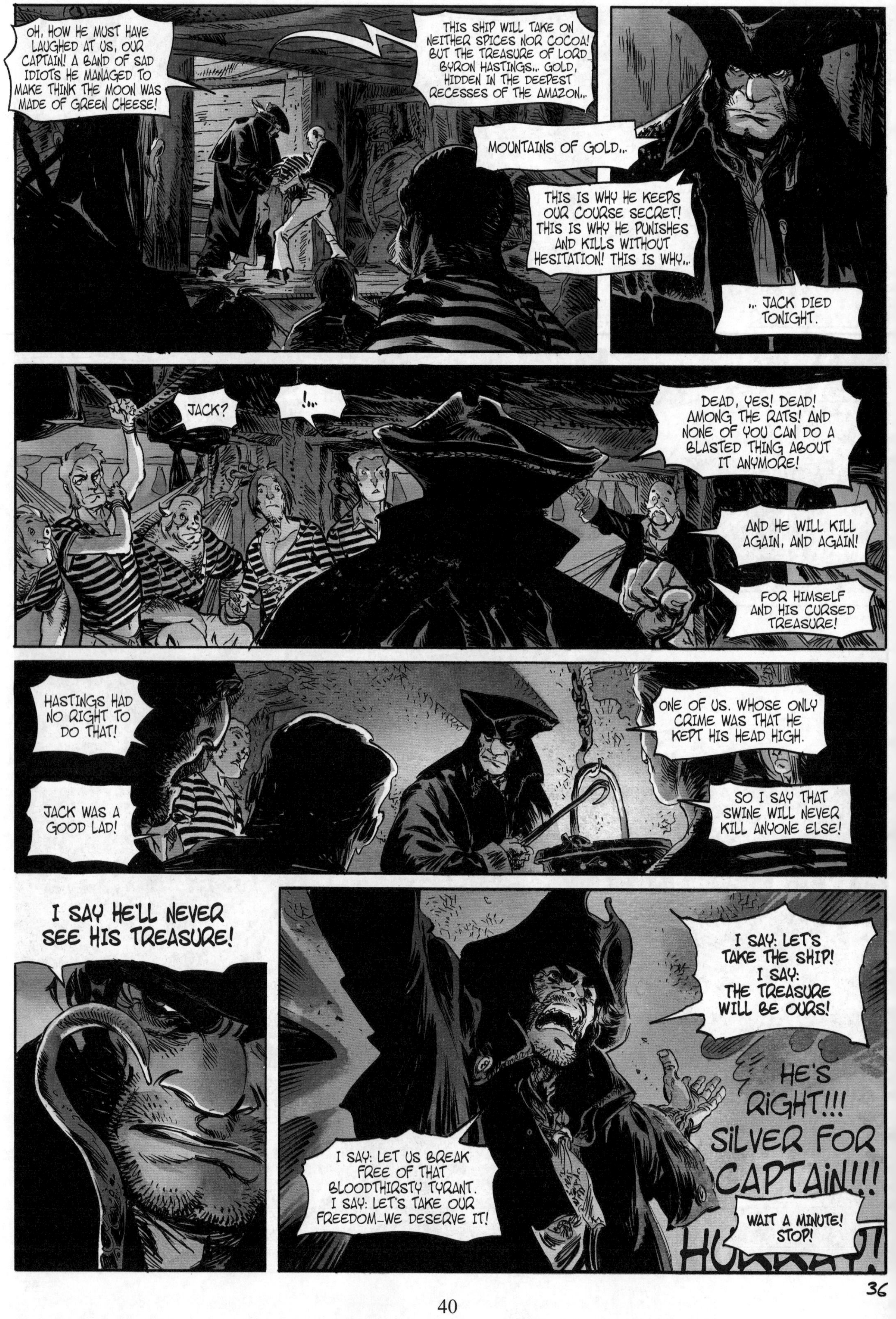
OH, HOW HE MUST HAVE LAUGHED AT US, OUR CAPTAIN! A BAND OF SAD IDIOTS HE MANAGED TO MAKE THINK THE MOON WAS MADE OF GREEN CHEESE!
THIS SHIP WILL TAKE ON NEITHER SPICES NOR COCOA! BUT THE TREASURE OF LORD BYRON HASTINGS... GOLD, HIDDEN IN THE DEEPEST RECESSES OF THE AMAZON...
MOUNTAINS OF GOLD...
THIS IS WHY HE KEEPS OUR COURSE SECRET! THIS IS WHY HE PUNISHES AND KILLS WITHOUT HESITATION! THIS IS WHY...
... JACK DIED TONIGHT.
JACK?
!...
DEAD, YES! DEAD! AMONG THE RATS! AND NONE OF YOU CAN DO A BLASTED THING ABOUT IT ANYMORE!
AND HE WILL KILL AGAIN, AND AGAIN!
FOR HIMSELF AND HIS CURSED TREASURE!
HASTINGS HAD NO RIGHT TO DO THAT!
JACK WAS A GOOD LAD!
ONE OF US. WHOSE ONLY CRIME WAS THAT HE KEPT HIS HEAD HIGH.
SO I SAY THAT SWINE WILL NEVER KILL ANYONE ELSE!
I SAY HE'LL NEVER SEE HIS TREASURE!
I SAY: LET'S TAKE THE SHIP! I SAY: THE TREASURE WILL BE OURS!
I SAY: LET US BREAK FREE OF THAT BLOODTHIRSTY TYRANT. I SAY: LET'S TAKE OUR FREEDOM—WE DESERVE IT!
HE'S RIGHT!!! SILVER FOR CAPTAIN!!!
WAIT A MINUTE! STOP!

36

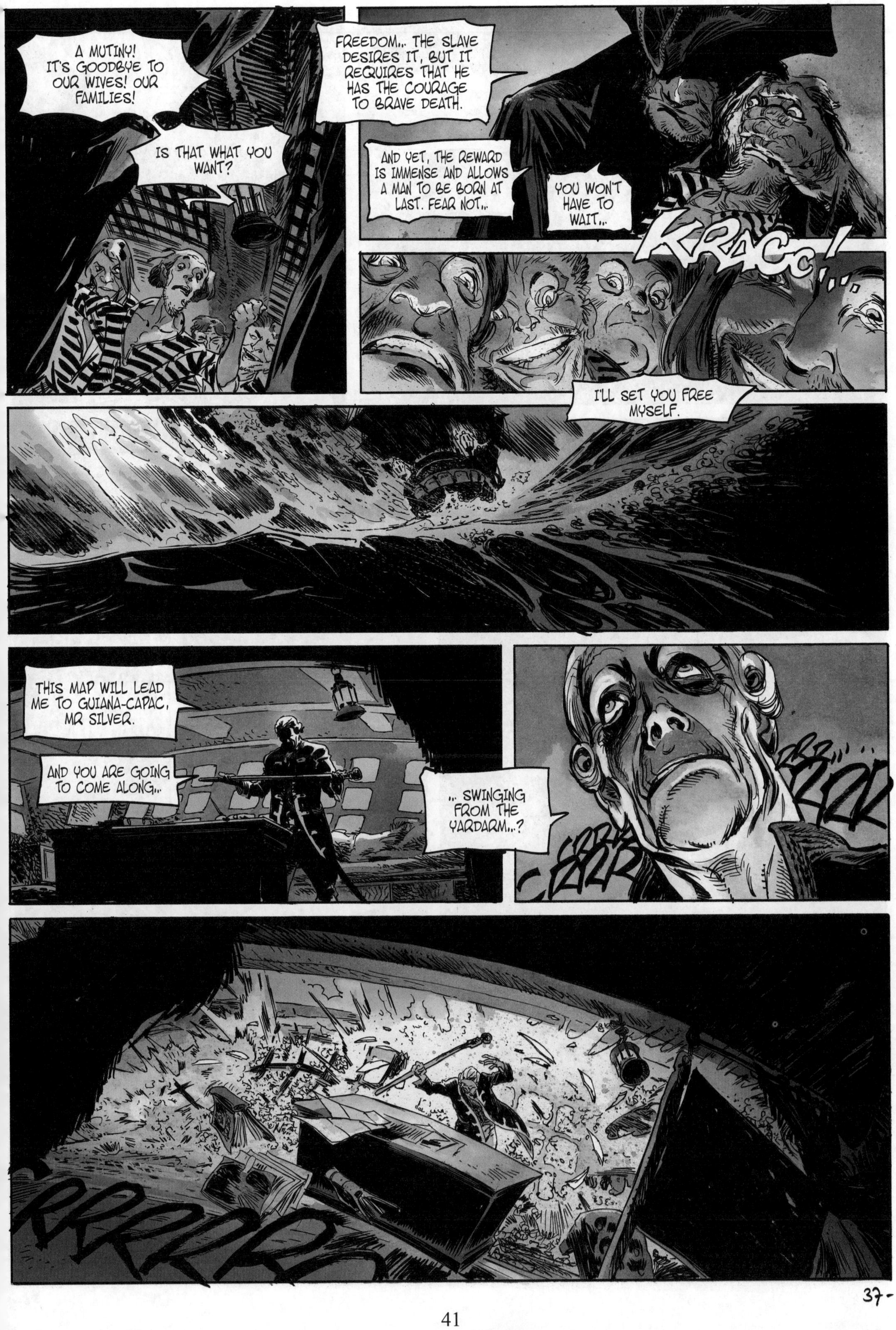
A MUTINY! IT'S GOODBYE TO OUR WIVES! OUR FAMILIES!
IS THAT WHAT YOU WANT?
FREEDOM... THE SLAVE DESIRES IT, BUT IT REQUIRES THAT HE HAS THE COURAGE TO BRAVE DEATH.
AND YET, THE REWARD IS IMMENSE AND ALLOWS A MAN TO BE BORN AT LAST. FEAR NOT...
YOU WON'T HAVE TO WAIT...
KRACC!
I'LL SET YOU FREE MYSELF.
THIS MAP WILL LEAD ME TO GUIANA-CAPAC, MR SILVER.
AND YOU ARE GOING TO COME ALONG...
... SWINGING FROM THE YARDARM...?
RRRR
CRRR
RRRRR

37-

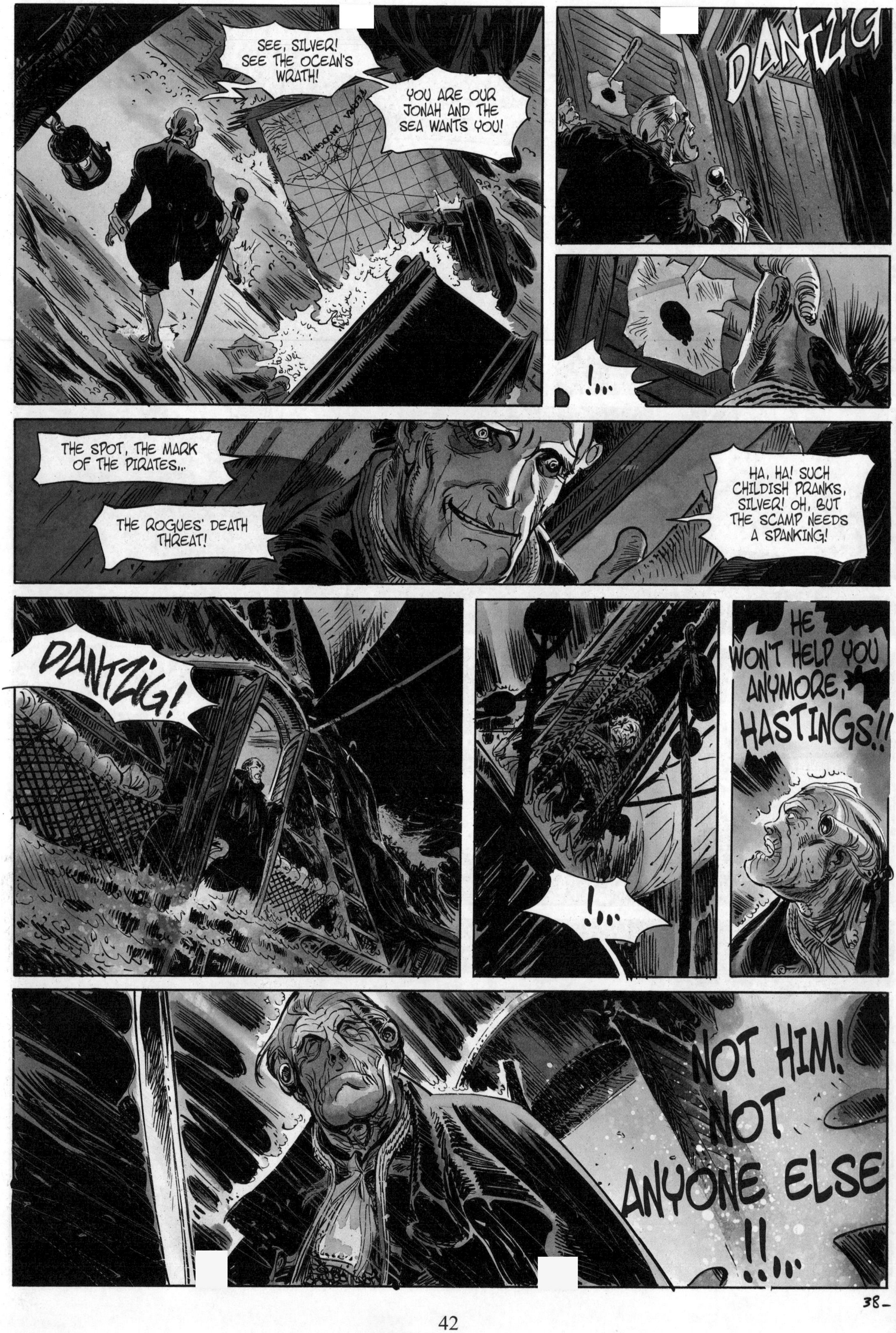
SEE, SILVER! SEE THE OCEAN'S WRATH!
YOU ARE OUR JONAH AND THE SEA WANTS YOU!
DANTZIG
!...
THE SPOT, THE MARK OF THE PIRATES...
THE ROGUES' DEATH THREAT!
HA, HA! SUCH CHILDISH PRANKS, SILVER! OH, BUT THE SCAMP NEEDS A SPANKING!
DANTZIG!
!...
HE WON'T HELP YOU ANYMORE, HASTINGS!!
NOT HIM! NOT ANYONE ELSE !!...
38

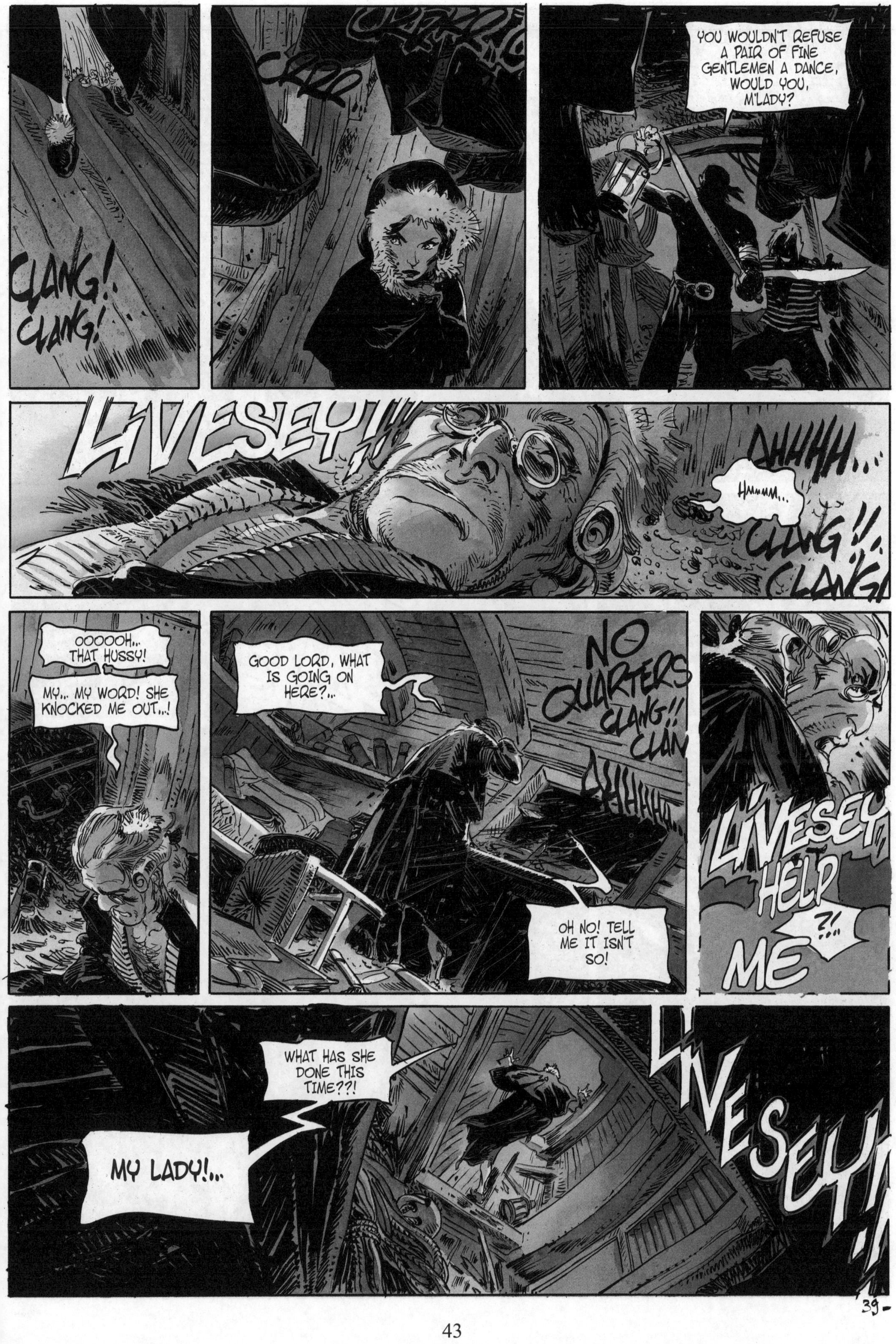
CLANG!
CLANG!
YOU WOULDN'T REFUSE A PAIR OF FINE GENTLEMEN A DANCE, WOULD YOU, M'LADY?
LIVESEY!!
OHHHH...
HMMMM...
CLANG!!
CLANG!
OOOOOH... THAT HUSSY!
MY... MY WORD! SHE KNOCKED ME OUT...!
GOOD LORD, WHAT IS GOING ON HERE?...
NO QUARTERS
CLANG!! CLAN
OH NO! TELL ME IT ISN'T SO!
LIVESEY
HELP ME
?!...
WHAT HAS SHE DONE THIS TIME??!
MY LADY!...
LIVESEY!!
39

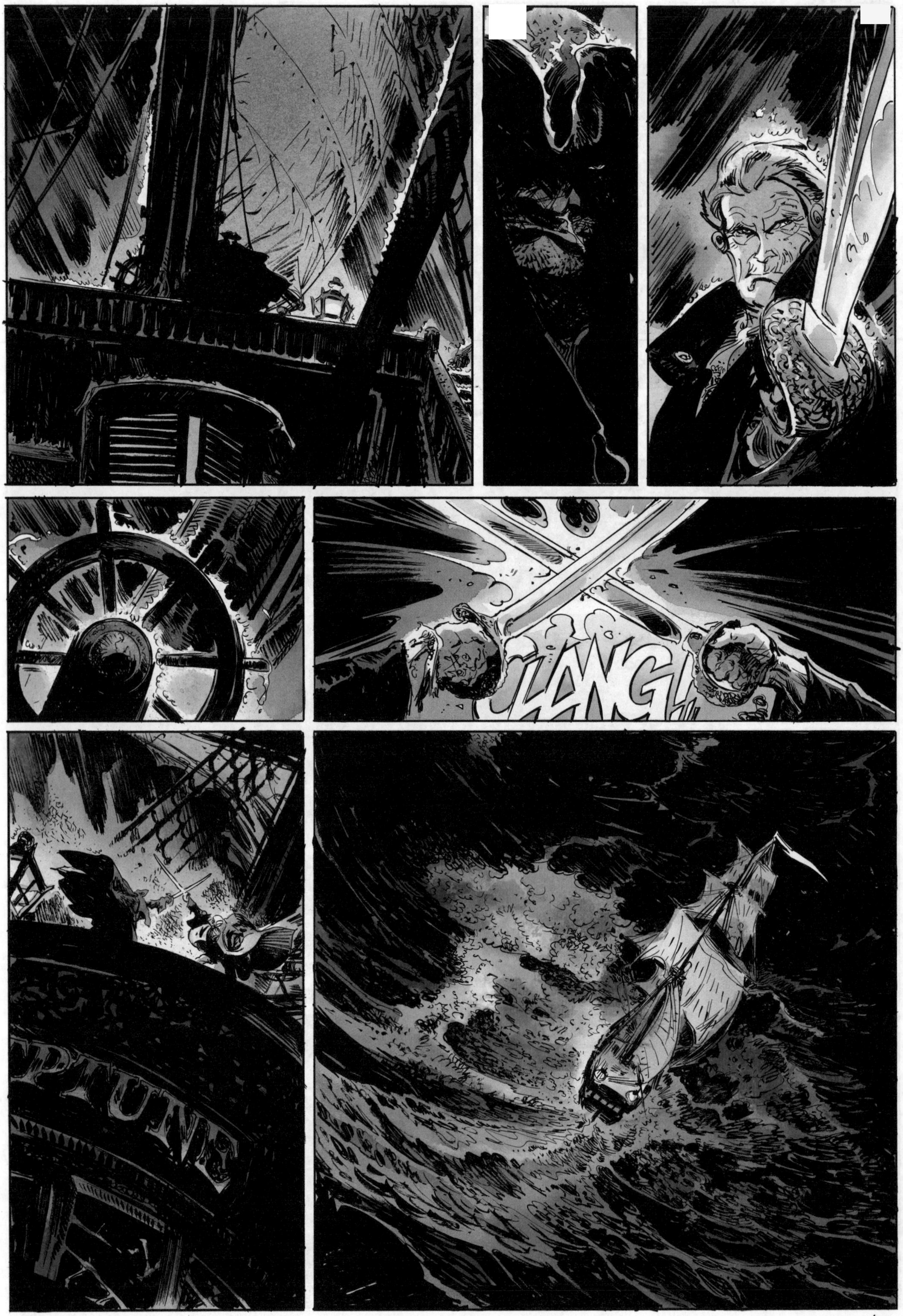
CLANG!

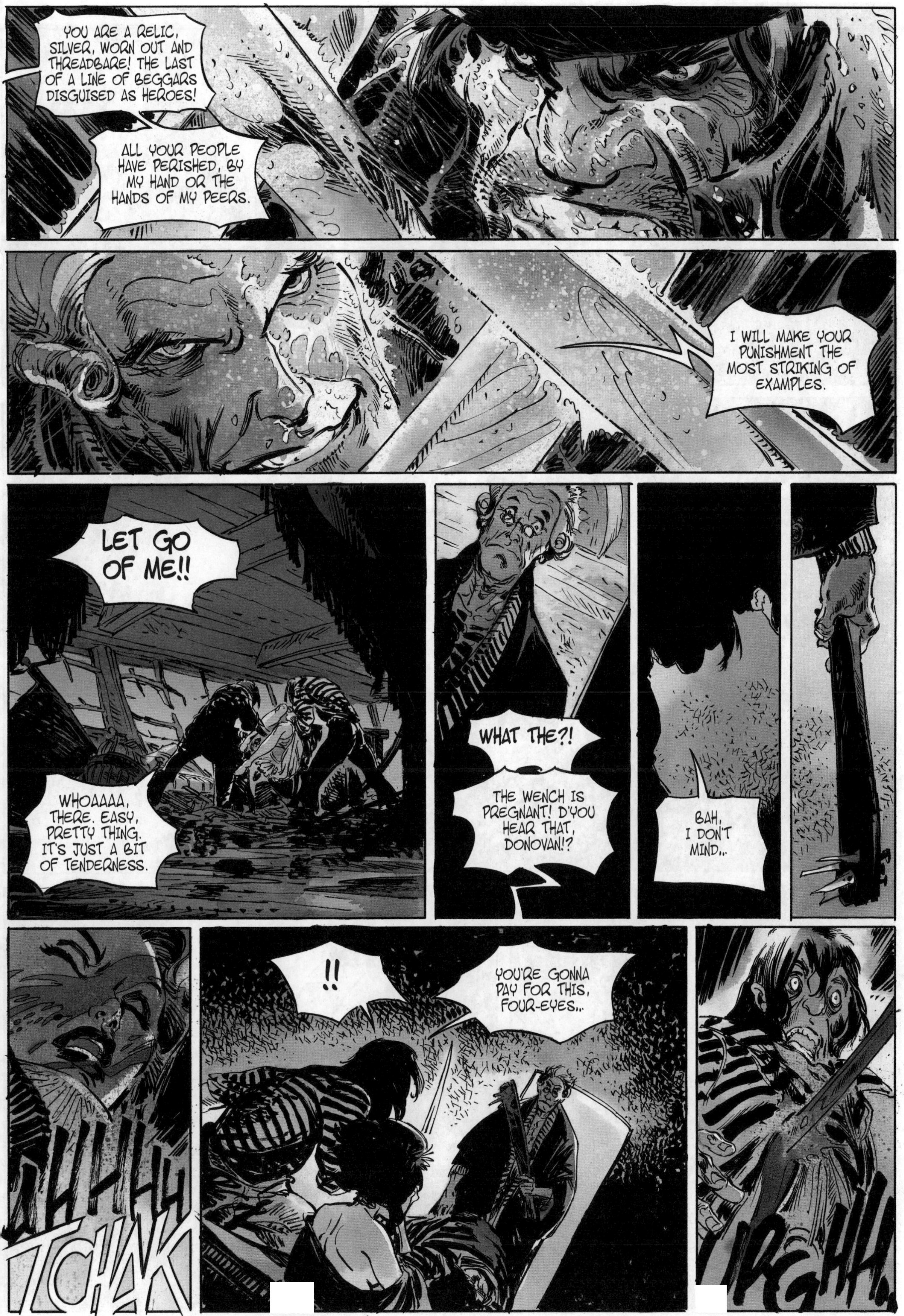
YOU ARE A RELIC, SILVER, WORN OUT AND THREADBARE! THE LAST OF A LINE OF BEGGARS DISGUISED AS HEROES!
ALL YOUR PEOPLE HAVE PERISHED, BY MY HAND OR THE HANDS OF MY PEERS.
I WILL MAKE YOUR PUNISHMENT THE MOST STRIKING OF EXAMPLES.
LET GO OF ME!!
WHOAAAA, THERE. EASY, PRETTY THING. IT'S JUST A BIT OF TENDERNESS.
WHAT THE?!
THE WENCH IS PREGNANT! D'YOU HEAR THAT, DONOVAN!?
BAH, I DON'T MIND...
TCHAK
!!
YOU'RE GONNA PAY FOR THIS, FOUR-EYES...
URGHH.

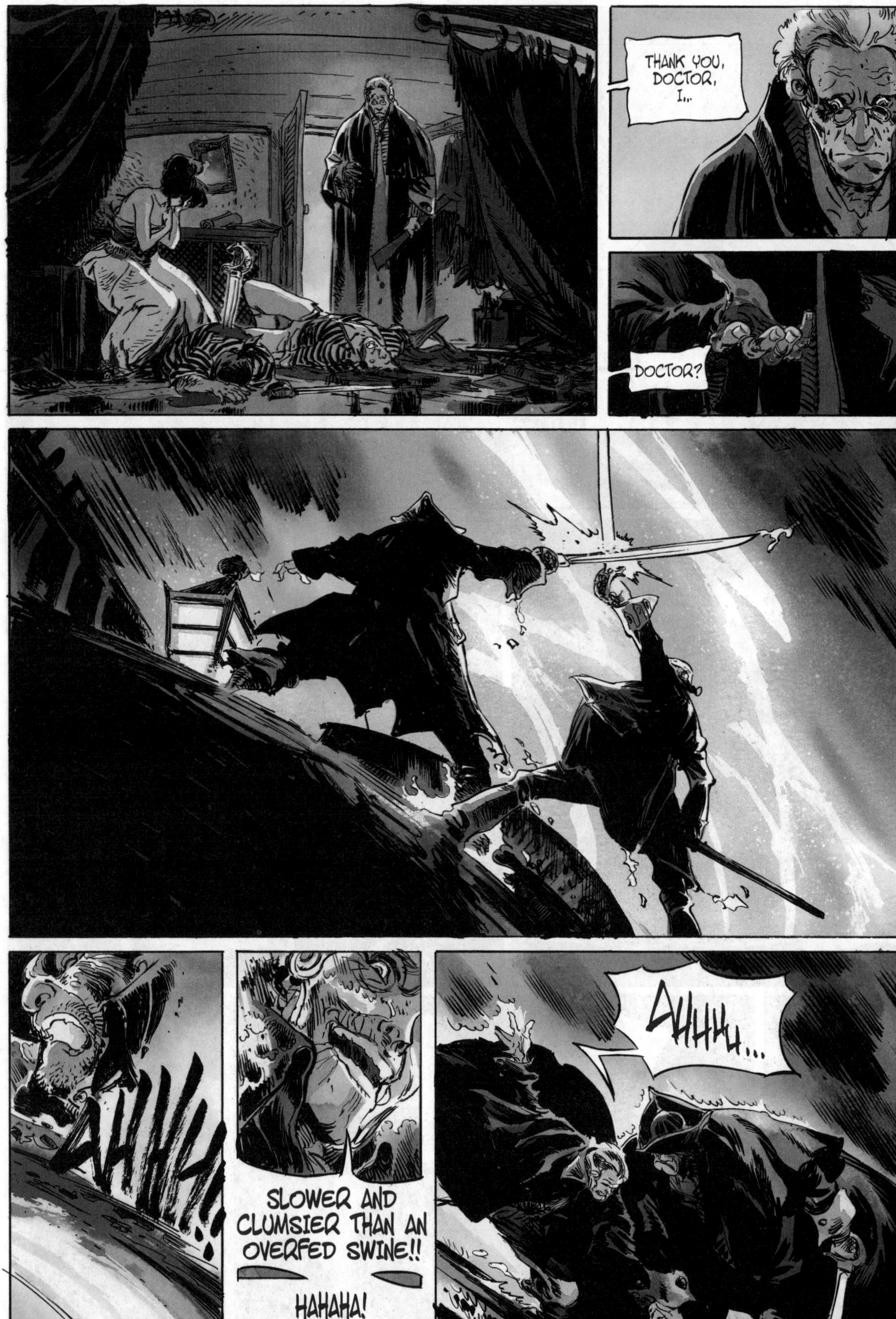
THANK YOU, DOCTOR, I...
DOCTOR?
AHHH!!
SLOWER AND CLUMSIER THAN AN OVERFED SWINE!!
HAHAHA! IS THIS THE GREAT SILVER?!
AHHH...

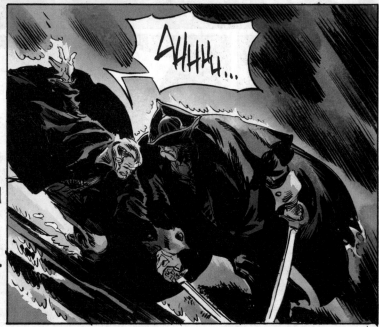

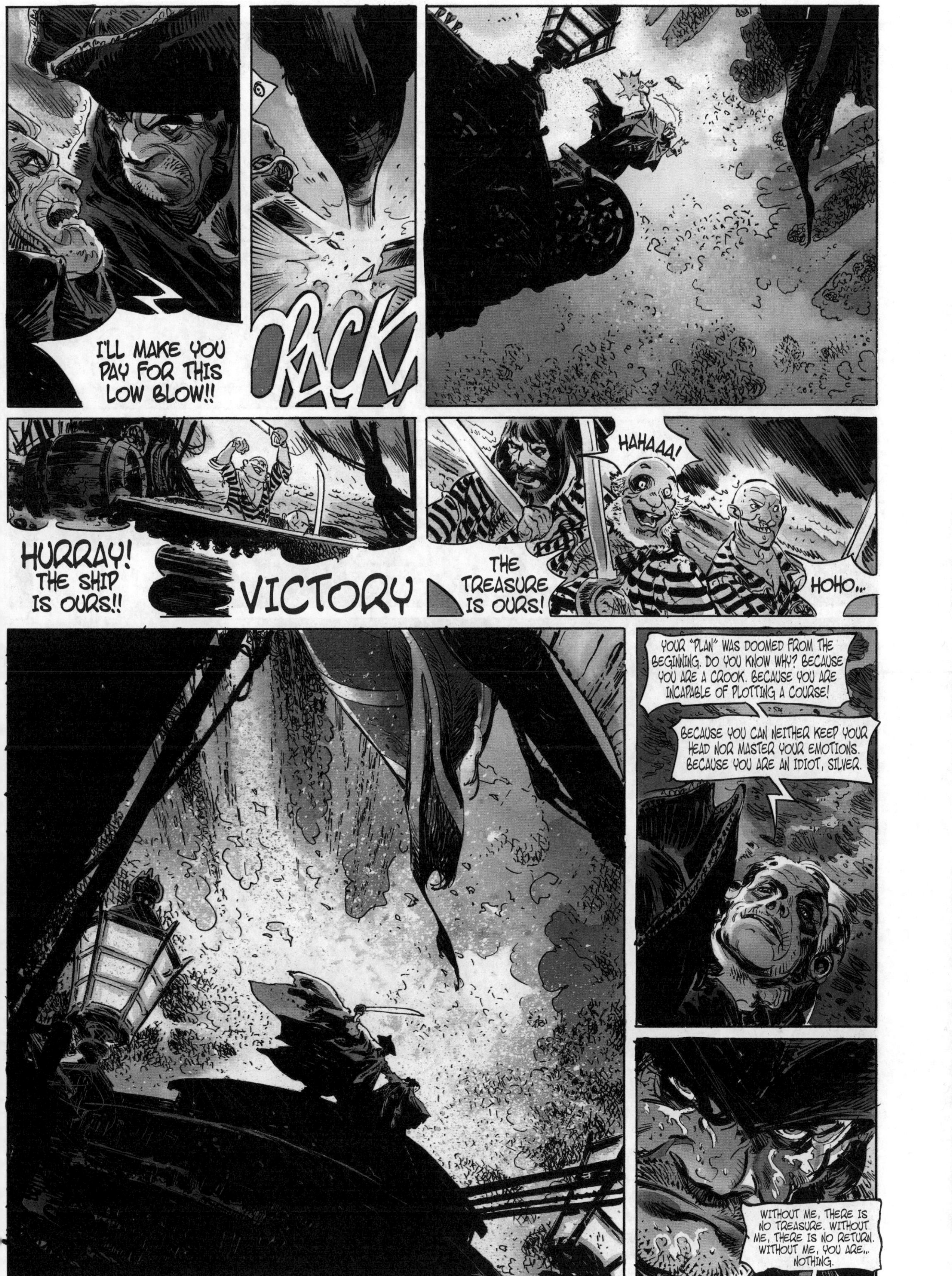
I'LL MAKE YOU PAY FOR THIS LOW BLOW!!
CRACK
HURRAY! THE SHIP IS OURS!!
VICTORY
HAHAAA!
THE TREASURE IS OURS!
HOHO...
YOUR "PLAN" WAS DOOMED FROM THE BEGINNING. DO YOU KNOW WHY? BECAUSE YOU ARE A CROOK. BECAUSE YOU ARE INCAPABLE OF PLOTTING A COURSE!
BECAUSE YOU CAN NEITHER KEEP YOUR HEAD NOR MASTER YOUR EMOTIONS. BECAUSE YOU ARE AN IDIOT, SILVER.
WITHOUT ME, THERE IS NO TREASURE. WITHOUT ME, THERE IS NO RETURN. WITHOUT ME, YOU ARE... NOTHING.
43-

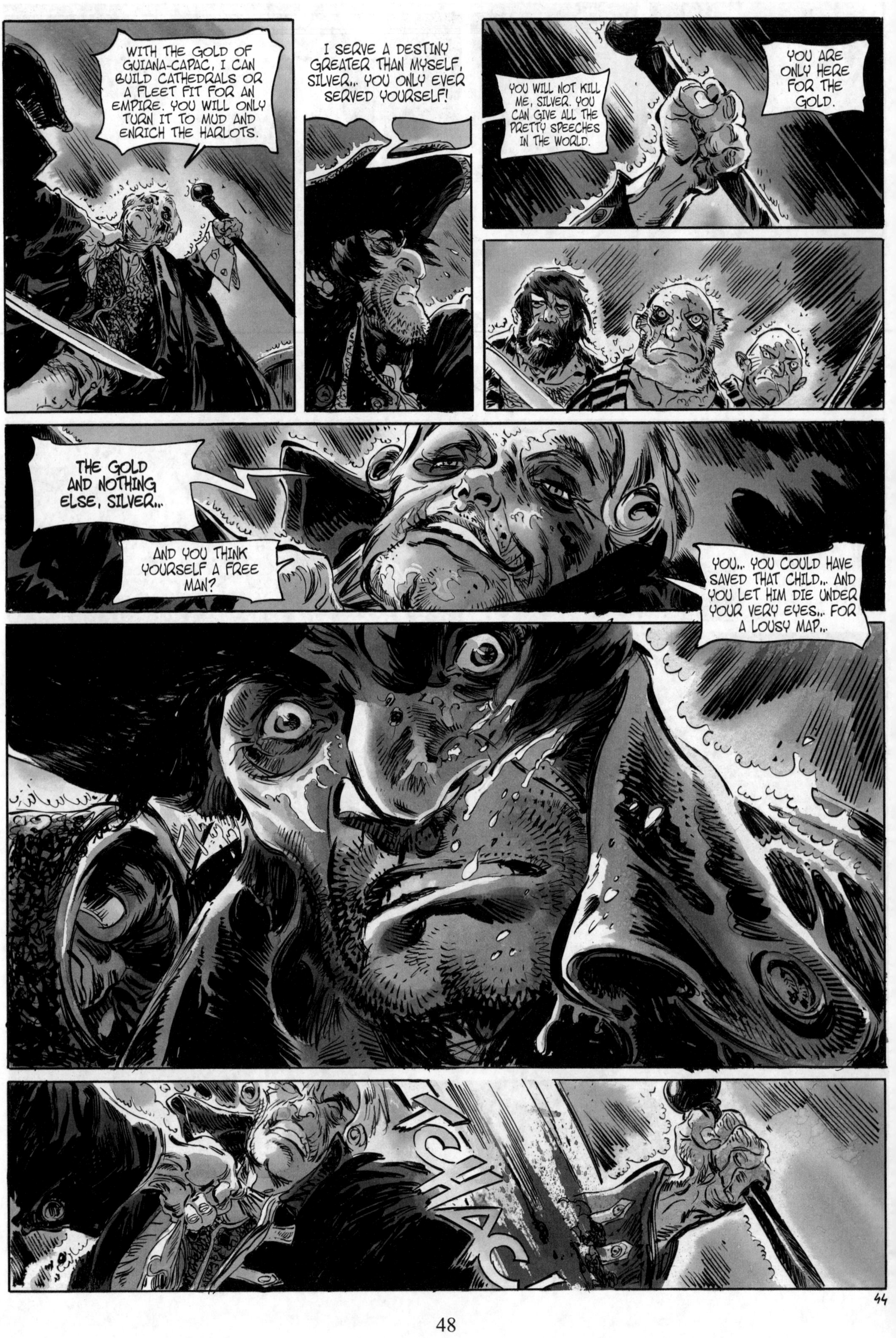
WITH THE GOLD OF GUIANA-CAPAC, I CAN BUILD CATHEDRALS OR A FLEET FIT FOR AN EMPIRE. YOU WILL ONLY TURN IT TO MUD AND ENRICH THE HARLOTS.
I SERVE A DESTINY GREATER THAN MYSELF, SILVER... YOU ONLY EVER SERVED YOURSELF!
YOU WILL NOT KILL ME, SILVER. YOU CAN GIVE ALL THE PRETTY SPEECHES IN THE WORLD.
YOU ARE ONLY HERE FOR THE GOLD.
THE GOLD AND NOTHING ELSE, SILVER...
AND YOU THINK YOURSELF A FREE MAN?
YOU... YOU COULD HAVE SAVED THAT CHILD... AND YOU LET HIM DIE UNDER YOUR VERY EYES... FOR A LOUSY MAP...

44

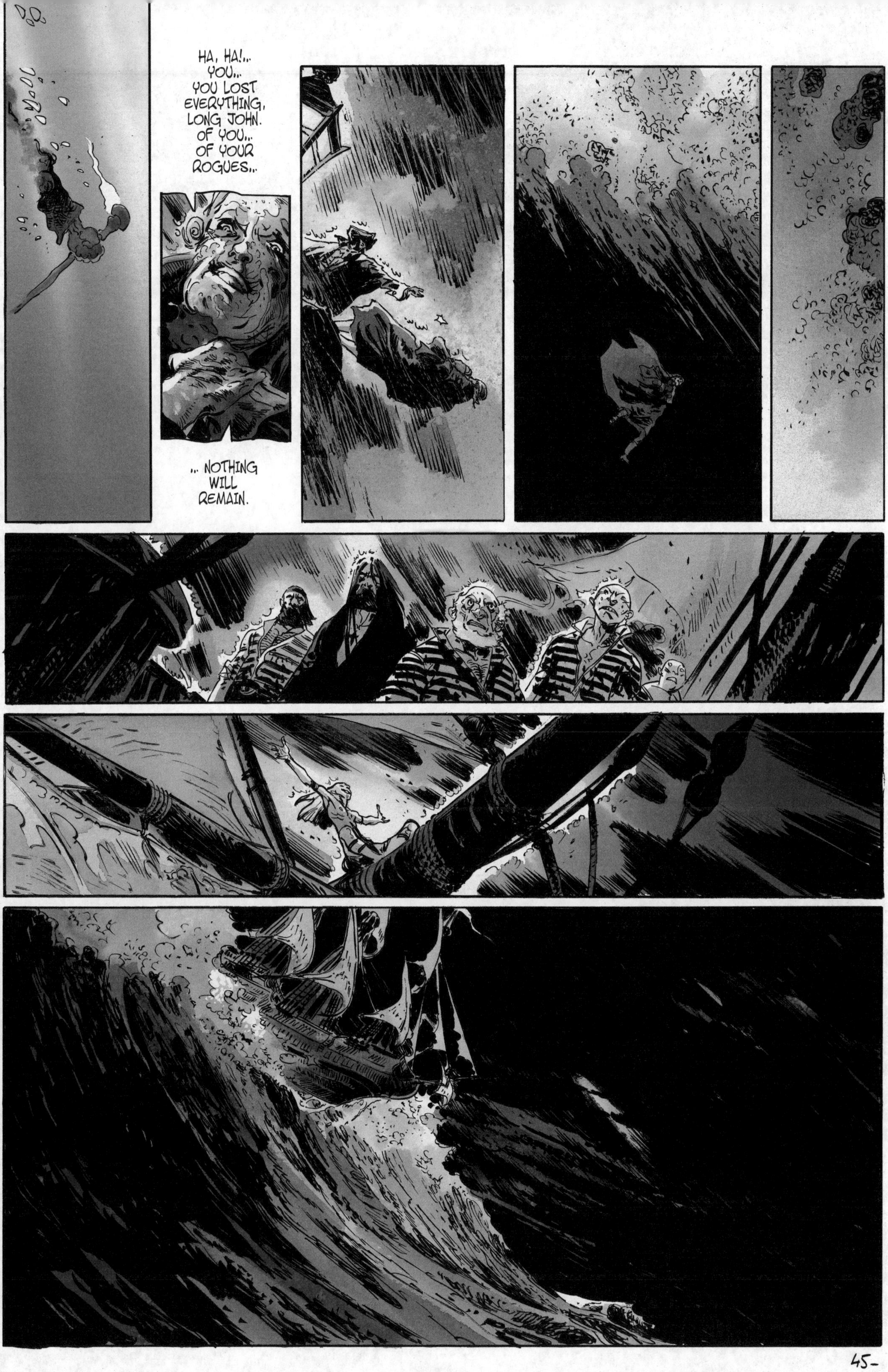
HA, HA!.. YOU.. YOU LOST EVERYTHING, LONG JOHN. OF YOU.. OF YOUR ROGUES..
.. NOTHING WILL REMAIN.
45-

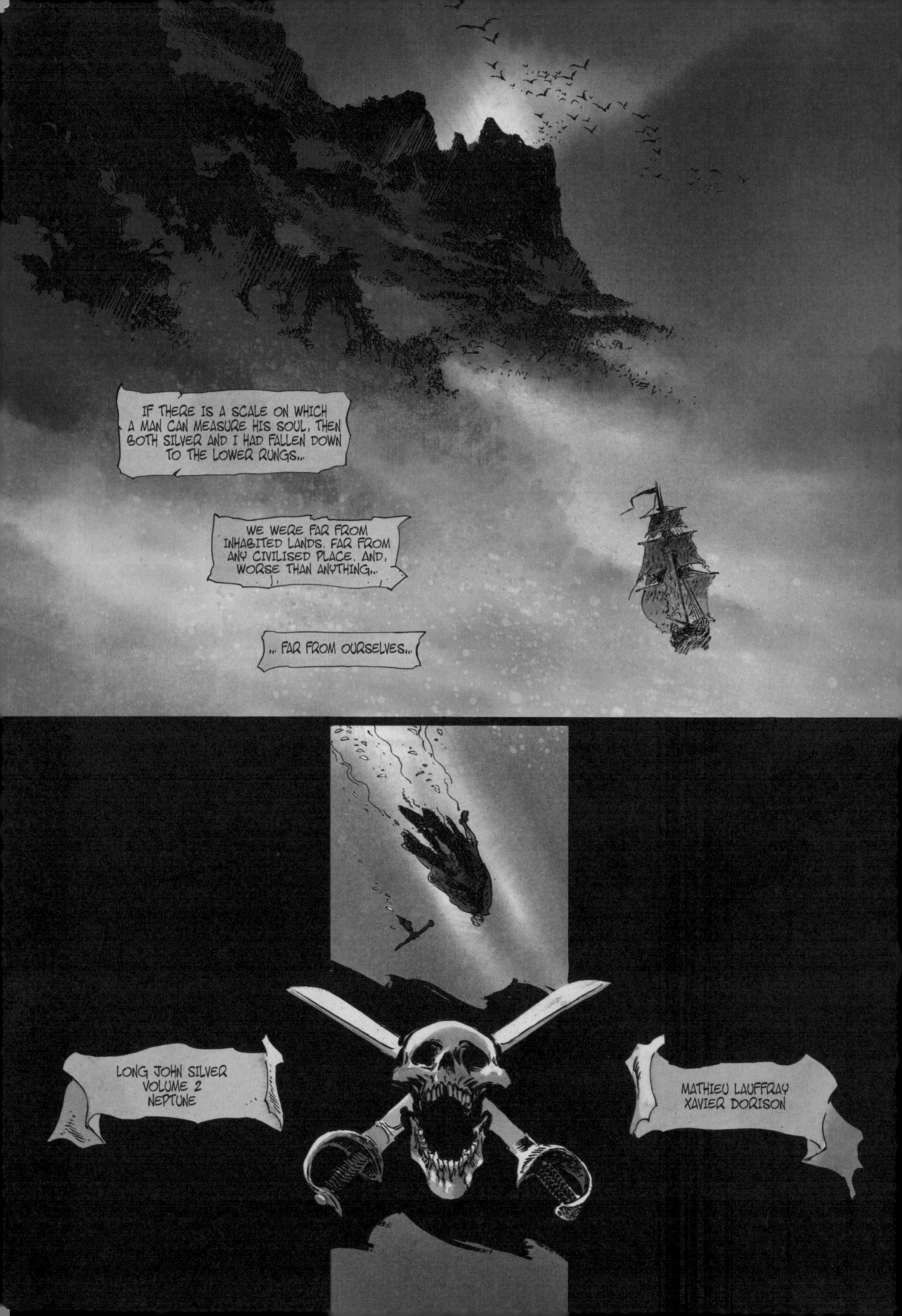
IF THERE IS A SCALE ON WHICH A MAN CAN MEASURE HIS SOUL, THEN BOTH SILVER AND I HAD FALLEN DOWN TO THE LOWER RUNGS...
WE WERE FAR FROM INHABITED LANDS. FAR FROM ANY CIVILISED PLACE. AND, WORSE THAN ANYTHING...
... FAR FROM OURSELVES...
LONG JOHN SILVER VOLUME 2 NEPTUNE
MATHIEU LAUFFRAY XAVIER DORISON

# LONG JOHN SILVER

THIS BOOK DOES NOT CLAIM TO BE A SEQUEL TO *TREASURE ISLAND*.
MERELY AN HOMAGE TO AN EXTRAORDINARY MASTERPIECE THAT HAS NEVER
STOPPED EVOKING WONDER IN US EVER SINCE WE WERE CHILDREN.
ITS ONE AND ONLY GOAL IS TO FIND AGAIN A BIT OF STARDUST FROM
THE GREAT DREAM THAT ROBERT LOUIS STEVENSON SPARKED…

## XAVIER DORISON

## MATHIEU LAUFFRAY

XAVIER DORISON IS ONE OF THE RISING STARS OF THE FRENCH COMIC SCENE. AUTHOR OF SEVERAL SUCCESSFUL SERIES SUCH AS "WEST," "SANCTUARY" AND "THE THIRD TESTAMENT," HE ALSO CO-WROTE THE SCRIPT OF THE FRENCH MOVIE "LES BRIGADES DU TIGRE."

MATHIEU LAUFFRAY DRAWS, AMONG OTHERS, THE SERIES "PROPHET." HE HAS WORKED AS A CONCEPT ARTIST FOR THE CINEMA ("BROTHERHOOD OF THE WOLF") AND VIDEO GAMES INDUSTRY ("ALONE IN THE DARK 4").

# LONG JOHN SILVER

Xavier
Dorison
Mathieu
Lauffray
Long John Silver
I - Lady Vivian Hastings

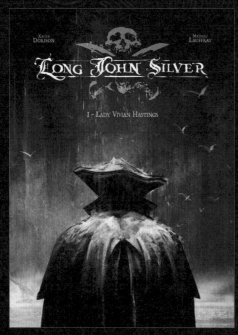

I - Lady Vivian Hastings

Xavier
Dorison
Mathieu
Lauffray
Long John Silver
II - Neptune

II - Neptune

COMING SOON

Xavier
Dorison
Mathieu
Lauffray
Long John Silver
III - The Emerald Maze

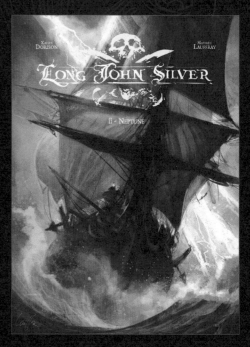

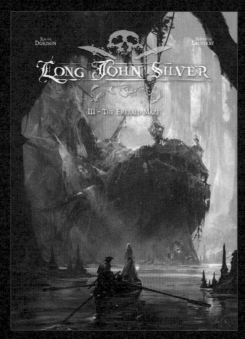

III - The Emerald Maze